25 WORDS & CAROLS
TO CELEBRATE ADVENT

THE WONDER OF CHRISTMAS

KEN PETERSEN
& RANDY PETERSEN

Our Daily Bread
Publishing.

The Wonder of Christmas: 25 Words and Carols to Celebrate Advent
© 2023 by Ken Petersen and Randy Petersen

Interior design by Jody Langley

ISBN: 978-1-64070-270-7

Library of Congress Cataloging-in-Publication Data Available

Printed in the United States of America
23 24 25 26 27 28 29 30 / 8 7 6 5 4 3 2 1

To Mom,
whose joy for caroling led us into the season

Contents

CONTENTS

Introduction

The two of us remember with hearty laughter the Christmas when Mom decided to buy all the family gifts at yard sales. Through the fall months, she went to garage sales and flea markets looking for novelties she could wrap and put under the tree. She felt it would be fun and less commercial.

Let's just say she went a little overboard. The result was an endless sea of packages covering the living room floor on Christmas Eve.

What really created the family memory, though, was that as Christmas approached, Mom felt uneasy that all her gifts to us were used and discarded from someone else's attic. It wasn't special enough, she felt. So, she went out to stores and bought us another set of gifts that were brand-new. We opened yard-sale gifts on Christmas Eve and then unwrapped brand-new gifts on Christmas morning.

By noon on Christmas Day, we were all exhausted from opening the abundance of gifts. "Are we done yet?" became the Christmas version of our vacation mantra, "Are we there yet?"

We teased Mom about that Christmas for years to come, but the heart-truth of it wasn't lost on us. Mom so loved us that she wanted to give us an amazing abundance of gifts and make it the best Christmas ever. In a way, it was.

Within this fond, funny family memory, we find an echo of the gospel. We especially like this wording of Ephesians 1:5–6 from *The Message*: "Long, long ago [God the Father] decided to adopt us into his family through Jesus Christ. (What pleasure he took in planning this!) He wanted us to enter into the celebration of his lavish gift-giving by the hand of his beloved Son."[1]

Advent is the traditional church season leading up to Christmas, but we might think of it as twenty-five days to enter into God's "lavish gift-giving." This book is written to walk you through the Advent season by exploring words and carols that open the gift of Christmas and give it deeper meaning. Each day's entry provides a biblical word study to chew on, a Christmas carol to ponder in a new way, and a devotional thought to lead you into the presence of God.

We think of *The Wonder of Christmas* as a daily devotional with Bible study depth. It's a way for you to set aside the commercial trappings of the season and immerse yourself in the spiritual meaning of Christmas.

Our prayer is that this little book might help you experience the lavish love of a God who just can't stop giving.

Ken Petersen and Randy Petersen

1
Angel

An angel of the Lord appeared to them, and the glory of the Lord shone around them, and they were terrified.

LUKE 2:9

We remember Christmases from our childhood when our grandparents made a long drive halfway across the country to be with us for the holidays. We were always thrilled to see them (though partly because of the presents they were bringing). Dad would get a call from them en route and report to us kids that they would be arriving "in six hours and twenty-four minutes." (He was always gleefully proud of being precise with times.) In an era before GPS and cell phones, Grandma and Grandpa Pete would update Dad from pay phones at rest stops along the turnpike. Periodically Dad would report to us their constantly revised time of arrival. Later, Mom, looking out the window and seeing their car pull into our driveway, would excitedly announce, "They're here!"

The prologue to the Christmas story is like that, a series of excited exclamations: "Jesus is coming!" And the bearers of these ETA announcements were angels. In Luke's gospel, fourteen verses mention angels in the first two chapters alone.

Who are these Christmas angels, and what does the Bible tell us about them?

Angel. The word simply means "messenger." Throughout the Bible, we find angels bringing news to humans, reports of how God feels or what he has planned. In the Old Testament, angels delivered encouragement to a runaway slave (Genesis 16:7–11; 21:17), stopped a donkey from carrying a freelance prophet on a bad trip (Numbers 22:21–25), and assured a reluctant Gideon that he was a "mighty warrior" (Judges 6:12). In the accounts of Christ's birth, angel messengers appeared to Zechariah, Mary, Joseph (three times), and the shepherds.

Few of the angels are named in Scripture—Gabriel, Michael—but most are not. When they show up, they generally have a human appearance, though there's often something bright and shining about them. Sometimes they look like people clothed in bright white.

The Bible is clear: God created angels. Paul writes, "In him all things were created: things in heaven and on earth, visible and invisible" (Colossians 1:16). Biblical scholar Wayne Grudem observes that the Bible "suggests that [angels] don't 'exist' in the same way we do."[2] Angels are spirits, though they can sometimes take on human form.

Do angels have wings? Most people think so, but the Bible never specifically mentions *angels* with wings. Two other types of heavenly creatures—cherubim and seraphim—are depicted with wings, but (contrary to popular belief) these are very different from Gabriel and his ilk.

Another common assumption is that each of us has a guardian angel. While angels in general may have a guarding function (Psalm 91:11–12), the Bible never describes those specific assignments. Yet angels do "serve" humans—"Are not all angels

ministering spirits sent to serve those who will inherit salvation?"
(Hebrews 1:14).

Sinclair Ferguson makes the observation of the angels at
Christmas, "It's clear that all these angels spoke the local language—which happens to have been Aramaic, a form of Hebrew.
Angels can speak in human tongues."[3] Which is an important skill
for messengers delivering the good news about the baby Jesus to
the whole world.

In our modern Christmas culture, angels are often romanti-
cized, cherubic figures of sweetness and light. But this is not how
biblical figures responded to them. An angel's opening line was
often "Don't be afraid"—so there was obviously something fright-
ening about them. Perhaps this was due to their brightness, their
otherworldly appearance, or the tone of their voice. Something
about them inspired fear in people.

Tim Keller sheds light on the fear we feel in the presence of
angels:

> The shepherds experienced terror before the angels,
> but it wasn't simply the fear of the uncanny. As with
> every other such appearance in the Bible, it was be-
> cause human beings are radically threatened by the
> presence of the holy. When God's glory appears, it
> always accentuates and intensifies our fundamental
> fearfulness because we are alienated from God. The
> angel, however, has an astonishing message: "You
> won't have to be afraid anymore if you look at what
> I am showing you." The fear that inhabits the deep
> place of our souls can be dispelled for good. How?
> The angels say, fear not—but look! (Luke 2:10).[4]

One often-forgotten Christmas carol references something else about angels.

"In the Bleak Midwinter" is a title that will never make the *Billboard* Hot 100, but it features two of the leading British artists of the 1800s. The sweet, melancholic tune was composed by Gustav Holst, known for his orchestral suite *The Planets*. And famed poet Christina Rossetti penned the hushed lyrics, showing the angels present at the birth of Jesus:

> Angels and archangels may have gathered there,
> Cherubim and seraphim thronged the air.

Indeed, these angelic messengers have another purpose: *they worship God.*

Preparing for Christmas

In the modern-day anticipation of Christmas that involves gift lists and Black Friday shopping binges, take some moments apart. Think of the angels announcing this remarkable event of God entering humanity to save us. Recapture some of the quiet mystery and, yes, awesome fear of those who encountered angels in the days leading up to Jesus's birth.

> *Lord God, in these moments of quiet, bring me back to the true anticipation of Christmas. Reignite in me the amazement that angels bring.*

In biblical times, like today, some people worshiped angels. Paul warned one church about this heresy (Colossians 2:18), which bore some resemblance to Gnosticism, which arose in the following century and claimed Jesus was just a rung on an angelic ladder leading to God. It's a mistake people have made throughout history, following the messenger and not the Messiah. This is probably why the book of Hebrews goes to great lengths to prove that Jesus is superior to angels (1:4–14), and why Revelation includes a scene where an angel scolds John for bowing to him: "Don't do that! I am a fellow servant with you and with your brothers and sisters who hold to the testimony of Jesus. Worship God!" (19:10).

2
Dream

*But after he had considered this, an angel of the Lord
appeared to him in a dream.*

MATTHEW 1:20

The advent of Christmas in the Bible begins with angels and dreams, sometimes at the same time.

We are told specifically that an angel appeared to Joseph in a dream, informing him of the remarkable event that was to take place and instructing him on how to handle it. Matthew also reports that the wise men, the magi, after visiting the Christ child, are warned in a dream not to report back to King Herod as they had promised (2:12). Then Joseph has another dream in which an angel tells him to move Mary and Jesus out of Herod's reach to Egypt (v. 13). Later, two more dreams direct the holy family back to Nazareth (vv. 19, 22).

In the first two chapters of the New Testament, five dreams are reported. They seem to be important in the Christmas story.

Today we think of dreams as a kind of wishful subconscious thinking, like an alternate version of real life that's essentially fictional. But dreams in the Bible seem to have a more solid reality and purpose.

In Genesis, Joseph lives and (nearly) dies by his dreams, first annoying his jealous brothers with visions of grandeur, then wowing the Egyptian pharaoh by nailing a dream interpretation. More than a millennium later, Daniel does much the same thing with a Babylonian king.

God spoke to a number of other prophets through visions, but these appear to be different from normal nighttime dreams. Two different Hebrew words are used for sleep dreams and prophetic visions. Yet the prophet Joel predicted a time when God would use both to communicate freely with all believers: "Your sons and daughters will prophesy, your old men will dream dreams, your young men will see visions" (2:28).

In the Bible, then, dreams and visions are ways in which God communicates with people.

So, as we engage with the gospel accounts of Jesus's birth, we might look at these dreams as something other than fanciful imagination or Freudian slips of subconscious reality. The gospel writers were reporting news events, and it's no accident that they presented these dreams alongside the facts of the events taking place. Certainly, Joseph and the magi believed these dreams to be reliable messages—they followed their advice and instruction to a tee.

We marvel that Mary and Joseph encountered dreams and angels, but let's not miss the message in our marvel about the method. The point of the Christmas story is really about God's *leading*—that Mary and Joseph followed the direction of God. This was against all reason, for Mary was a virgin and none of it looked good socially. Mary doubted and Joseph was beside himself, and yet they followed the direction of God that came to them through angels and dreams.

A little-known traditional carol, simply titled "The Boy's Dream," tells of a young boy going to sleep to the voice of an angel retelling the Christmas story:

> I heard his sweet voice caroling,
> Full softly in my ear,
> A song for Christian boys to sing,
> For Christian men to hear.

The carol is a lullaby, soft and sweet, echoing the Christmas story of angels and dreams. Yet it doesn't miss the message. The carol concludes with a prayer of hope that this boy will grow up to be like Jesus:

> Like Him be true, like Him be pure,
> Like Him be full in love.[5]

Those lyrics echo a passage in Philippians: "Finally, brothers and sisters, whatever is true, whatever is noble, whatever is right, whatever is pure, whatever is lovely, whatever is admirable—if anything is excellent or praiseworthy—think about such things. Whatever you have learned or received or heard from me, or seen in me—put it into practice. And the God of peace will be with you" (4:8–9).

The message of Christmas is not angels or dreams but that Jesus is here and wants to be with us. He wants us to walk with him, talk with him.

The message of Christmas ultimately leads us, calls us, to be like Jesus.

Preparing for Christmas

So how does God connect with you? Perhaps it's not through angels or dreams, as the carol suggests, but through the counsel of a friend or the message from a pastor, or through the Scripture itself. Whatever the method, what is God telling you? How is he leading you?

Think about using this Advent time to discern how God is leading you. Maybe God is beckoning you to align your life differently. Maybe he wants you to "grow up" to be like Jesus. For you, what would that look like?

> *Lord God, help me enter into this Christmas season*
> *with a renewed sense of commitment to put some things*
> *into practice. Help me "like you be true, like you be*
> *pure, like you be full of love."*

It's interesting to note the parallels of dreams in Scripture. Matthew had an eye for the details of the Hebrew Scriptures, and he never shied away from showing how Jesus fit right into God's enduring plan.

The Joseph of Genesis did his dream reading in Egypt, and Mary's Joseph has a dream sending him to Egypt.

Daniel interpreted dreams for a Babylonian king, and the magi—very likely from Babylon ("the east") and possibly the heirs of a wisdom tradition started by Daniel—are warned in a dream to avoid the Judean king.

3

Virgin

*The virgin's name was Mary. The angel went
to her and said, "Greetings, you who are
highly favored! The Lord is with you."*

LUKE 1:27–28

Make no mistake: the Bible clearly reports that Jesus was born of a virgin. Both Matthew and Luke make that a key element of their nativity stories.

In Luke, Mary protests that she can't possibly give birth because she hasn't been with a man. "With God all things are possible," the angel replies (see 1:37).

That same sense of impossibility arises in Matthew as Joseph assumes his fiancée must have been unfaithful, and yet he looks for a way to call off the marriage quietly to minimize her dishonor. In a dream he learns that God has done the impossible.

Skeptics have long had difficulty accepting the virgin birth, and it's hard to blame them, because Mary and Joseph started out as skeptics too: "'How will this be,' Mary asked the angel, 'since I am a virgin?'" (Luke 1:34).

But Christianity is built on miracles, which are by definition things that are hard to believe (the Latin *mira* means "wonder"). The Bible is a record of God doing impossible things. Our very faith in God is based on the idea of the supernatural. Is the virgin birth too much for our God to do?

Matthew reminds us that the virgin birth was even foretold by Isaiah. "Therefore the Lord himself will give you a sign: The virgin will conceive and give birth to a son, and will call him Immanuel" (Isaiah 7:14; see Matthew 1:23).

This was God's plan from the beginning.

In the last century, there was quite a brouhaha when a new translation of the Bible referred to a "young woman" in Isaiah 7:14, not a "virgin" (as the King James Version had said for centuries). Were these scholars denying the virgin birth? Not really. The story of this translation teaches us not only about language but also about the way biblical prophecy works.

Isaiah used a Hebrew word (*alma*) that can refer to a virgin, but it can also be used for any young woman regardless of her sexual history. In ambiguous cases, translators look at context. The problem is, like many biblical prophecies, Isaiah 7:14 has two very different contexts. In Isaiah's time, God was giving a sign to the disbelieving King Ahaz, who was overreacting to some minor threats at his borders. A young woman would become a mother, and before that child was old enough to know right from wrong, those threats would vanish. That was God's assurance to Ahaz. Who was the young woman? Many scholars think she was Isaiah's own wife, whose childbirth is mentioned in the next chapter.

Of course, the second context of this prophecy is the virgin birth of Jesus some seven hundred years later.

King Ahaz would surely have thought Isaiah was talking about a normal birth by a young mother and not a miraculous virgin birth. And so modern translators, who try to present each statement *as its original hearers would understand it*, could legitimately render this as "young woman."

But here's another wrinkle. The Hebrew Scriptures were translated into Greek about a century before Jesus's birth. This Greek version, known as the Septuagint, used the word *parthenos*, a specific word for "virgin." (The Parthenon in Athens was named for the famous virgin goddess Athena.)

So as Matthew sets about writing the story of Jesus, leafing through his Greek version of Isaiah, he finds the verse that precisely explains what happened with Mary: a virgin conceived and bore a son, who became a sign of God's power for all eternity.

The gospel writers Matthew and Luke make a pretty big deal about the virgin birth. Why?

It's the cornerstone of a very important theology—that of the dual nature of Jesus Christ. He was God, but he also was man. His divine nature came from his eternal place in the Trinity, his "God-ness." His human nature, his physical being, came from Mary.

The virgin birth of Jesus Christ preserved his sinless divine nature while incarnating him in the flesh and blood of a human being. This became adopted by the early church creeds as the basis of Christian faith:

> I believe in God, the Father almighty,
>   creator of heaven and earth.
> I believe in Jesus Christ, his only Son, our Lord,
>   who was conceived by the Holy Spirit
>   and born of the virgin Mary.

We do not fully understand how the virgin birth actually works, of course, but that doesn't mean we can't believe in it. Some things are beautiful in their mystery.

If you ever have come upon the original version of "O Come, All Ye Faithful" (it's been revised and added to over the centuries), you may have shaken your head at one of the lyrics:

> God of God, light of light,
> Lo, He abhors not the virgin's womb;
> Very God, begotten, not created:
> O come, let us adore Him.

That second line is puzzling and makes a strong contender for online lists of "Strangest Christmas Carol Lyrics Ever." What is "abhors not the virgin's womb" supposed to mean?

Pastor and author A. W. Tozer offers a possible interpretation:

> The incarnation . . . was not something that Jesus Christ did gritting His teeth and saying, "I hate this thing—I wish I could get out of it." One of the dear old hymn writers said, "He abhorred not the virgin's womb." The writer thought about this and said, "Wait a minute here. The womb of the creature? How could the everlasting, eternal, infinite God, whom space cannot contain, confine Himself inside one of His creatures? Wouldn't it be a humiliation?" Then he smiled and said, "No, He abhorred not the virgin's womb," and he wrote it and we've been singing it for centuries."[6]

Strange lyrics aside, let's not lose sight of how concisely "O Come, All Ye Faithful" describes the virgin birth and dual nature of Christ. In just a few words, the theological beauty of the virgin birth is captured.

Preparing for Christmas

Take a moment to ponder the mystery and beauty of what the virgin birth accomplished. This ensured Jesus could be both God and man. It allowed him to walk in our shoes, endure our physical limitations, suffer our physical longings.

When you come to God in prayer, expressing your life challenges, be assured that he knows what it's like to be you.

Thank you, God, for sending your divine Son to become human, to know these things I am experiencing now.

God is our refuge and strength,
an ever-present help in trouble.

Psalm 46:1 NIV

Thank You
for requesting this resource

It's our hope that our resources bless you and draw you closer to God each day. We are so thankful for your prayers and support of our ministry.

Your friends at
Our Daily Bread Ministries

4
Mary

In a loud voice [Elizabeth] exclaimed: "Blessed are you among women, and blessed is the child you will bear! But why am I so favored, that the mother of my Lord should come to me?"

LUKE 1:42–43

Seven women are named Mary in the New Testament (though there may be some overlaps). You're probably familiar with Mary Magdalene and Mary the sister of Martha, but the one you want to read about this Advent season is the virgin Mary, the mother of Jesus.

Mary is a form of the Hebrew *Miriam*, the name of Moses's sister, a key player in the exodus from Egypt and the early leadership of the nation of Israel. Miriam was one of the most prominent women in the Old Testament, which might explain why so many women were named after her in the New. In Hebrew, the name Miriam/Mary is similar to the word for "rebellious"—which is more appropriate than you might think for both Miriam and Mary.

As a girl, Miriam helped her mother in the plot to keep baby Moses alive, despite the murderous intent of the Egyptian pharaoh (Exodus 2:1–10). Later, after the crossing of the Red Sea, Miriam led the women of Israel in a victorious song and dance number, celebrating the fall of their oppressors (15:21).

Like her Old Testament namesake, Mary also raised a song of rebellion, about how God "has brought down rulers from their thrones but has lifted up the humble" (Luke 1:52). Like baby Moses, the infant Jesus was whisked away from danger (escaping into Egypt), thwarting the violent designs of a wicked ruler (Matthew 2:14–15).

Who was Mary, this girl of Nazareth? The New Testament provides very little background, though many legends have arisen through the centuries. Most of what we really know comes from what the Bible says she did or said.

When Gabriel gave her the news that would overturn her life, she had some questions, but ultimately she trusted what God was doing: "I am the Lord's servant" (Luke 1:38). After traveling to Bethlehem, laying her newborn in a manger, and hearing shepherds babble about a heavenly host, she "treasured up all these things and pondered them in her heart" (2:19).

Mary's inner life soon became the subject of a statement by the prophet Simeon as he blessed Jesus in the temple. After predicting that this baby would "cause the falling and rising of many in Israel," he added a personal note for Mary: "And a sword will pierce your own soul too" (vv. 34–35). Many see this cryptic comment as a reference to Mary watching Jesus die on the cross, and it could be, but it might mean something broader. Raising the Messiah wouldn't be easy, and Mary might go through her own "falling and rising" over the years.

On a later trip to Jerusalem, when Jesus was twelve years old, Mary behaved like any mother, scolding him for lagging behind (v. 48). Perhaps she learned something from his response, though, as he talked about his need to be in his Father's house, involved in his Father's business. He wasn't talking about Joseph's workshop. He had a greater Father, a higher calling.

In our next glimpse of Mary, at the wedding in Cana, she shows a keen awareness of Jesus's calling. She actually calls him into his first miracle when he turns water to wine (John 2:1–11). But there's a later event that suggests some conflict. Crowds were following Jesus, making it difficult for him to take a lunch break. Some of his family members arrived to take him home, saying, "He is out of his mind" (Mark 3:21). But when Jesus was told that his mother and brothers were trying to get through the crowd, he looked around at the crowd and said, "Here are my mother and my brothers! Whoever does God's will is my brother and sister and mother" (vv. 34–35). Was he declaring independence from his family? And how did Mary feel about this? As if a sword were piercing her soul?

Other than these events, Mary is not mentioned during most of Jesus's ministry, though we might imagine she followed him around as others did. Notably, she's there at the foot of the cross, where Jesus tenderly asks his disciple John to care for her (John 19:26–27).

We may be rightly careful of not exalting Mary too much, but we should not miss the truth that she was remarkable for being unremarkable: she was an ordinary woman in an ordinary place and time—called by an extraordinary God.

Rebecca McLaughlin writes, "The first person to hear the good news about Jesus was a low-income teenage girl from a Podunk town. . . . This girl had the most common name of her day—a name belonging to one in five Jewish women of her time and place. She was just another Mary."

Mary was one of us, one of the common folk, not of wealth or royalty. Yet she was the choice of God to work a miracle.

McLaughlin continues: "[Mary] carried in her womb the one through whom all wombs were made. She nursed the one who generated life on earth. She reared the one who formed the stars. But as we look at Jesus through his mother's eyes, we see how God grabs ordinary folk to be his chosen agents in this world. When you and I let Jesus in, our humdrum lives become the buzzing center of a miracle—however little it may feel that way at times."[7]

Preparing for Christmas

Rather few Christmas carols focus on Mary primarily, most providing her just brief mentions as being present with the Christ child. But one carol gives her her due: "Mary of the Incarnation" tells the story of Christ as seen through her life.[8] The song is traditionally sung to the very familiar tune of Beethoven's "Ode to Joy."

Its opening words depict Mary in her ordinary human circumstances:

> Mary of the incarnation,
> youthful mother of her King,
> listening, trusting, travelling, working. . . .

Perhaps you identify with Mary—not because she was extraordinary but because she was ordinary like all of us. Yet she was open to the remarkable thing God called her to. Are you?

> *Lord God, provide me a view of Jesus through*
> *Mary's eyes. I want to respond to him in wonder*
> *and in faith as she did. Help me to be open to*
> *what you have for me to do.*

5
Christ

*The Spirit of the Lord is on me, because he has anointed
me to proclaim good news to the poor.*

LUKE 4:18

Many people today assume that "Christ" is just Jesus's last name: John Smith, meet Jesus Christ. That's not exactly right, but it's not far off. Among the early believers, the name "Jesus Christ" came together, sometimes with "Lord" attached. We see it throughout the New Testament. Yet Christ wasn't just a surname—it was a title, rich with significance and forecast long before the advent of Jesus Christ.

When Saul became Israel's first king, the prophet Samuel "took a flask of olive oil and poured it on Saul's head" (1 Samuel 10:1). That might seem an odd way to honor a monarch, but it had powerful symbolic meaning. Anointing, as it was called, became God's way of designating people for certain leadership positions.

A few years later, when Saul had worn out his welcome, Samuel went searching for another king—and found a shepherd boy named David. After his anointing, Scripture says, "The Spirit of the LORD came powerfully upon David" (16:13).

27

Not only kings but also some priests and prophets got the oil-on-the-head treatment as a sign of the Spirit's empowering and their commissioning for the service of God.

As time went on, the term "anointed one" appeared occasionally in Hebrew literature, referring to a leader empowered to do God's work, sometimes Israel's king (Psalm 2:2), sometimes a foreign king (Isaiah 45:1), sometimes a future king (Daniel 9:25). In Hebrew, it's a single word, *messiah* (the verb "anoint" is *masah*).

The latter part of Isaiah has several prophecies about someone who would be sent by God to serve and to suffer. That person says,

> The Spirit of the Sovereign LORD is on me,
>   because the LORD has anointed [*masah*] me
>   to proclaim good news to the poor.
> He has sent me to bind up the brokenhearted,
>   to proclaim freedom for the captives
>   and release from darkness for the prisoners,
> to proclaim the year of the LORD's favor
>   and the day of vengeance of our God,
> to comfort all who mourn. (61:1–2)

When Jesus began his public ministry, standing up to read the Scripture in his home synagogue, this is the passage he read. And he added, "Today this scripture is fulfilled in your hearing" (Luke 4:21). This caused an uproar, because the people knew what he was saying (without exactly saying it): "I am the Anointed One Isaiah was talking about."

The Greek word for "anoint" is *chrio*. For "anointed one," it's *christos*. So when the angel told the shepherds of Bethlehem that the baby in the manger was "Christ the Lord" (Luke 2:11 KJV), it meant that this was the Messiah, the Anointed One, the leader Isaiah and others had prophesied about, who was empowered by

God's Spirit to bring in a season of God's favor, to heal broken hearts.

All of that, wrapped up in swaddling clothes.

Jesus did not go around saying, "I'm the Messiah." That would have surely ignited a fury that would have ended his ministry too soon. He did, however, let others say it for him, though he often told them to be discreet about it. As a result, many people thought he was merely a popular rabbi, perhaps a prophet, maybe even a reincarnation of one of the prophets of old.

So when Jesus asked his disciples point-blank who they thought he was, and Peter answered, "You are the Christ, the Son of the living God" (Matthew 16:16 NKJV), Jesus blessed him profusely. Apparently Peter really was paying attention. He had come to recognize that Jesus was the Anointed One.

A Christmas song that echoes these Christ themes is one you might not know: "Hail to the Lord's Anointed." Written by a Scottish newspaper editor, James Montgomery, its lyrics are based on Psalm 72.

Consider the first verses of that psalm:

> Endow the king with your justice, O God,
>   the royal son with your righteousness.
> May he judge your people in righteousness,
>   your afflicted ones with justice. (vv. 1–2)

This psalm is attributed to Solomon, yet scholars aren't sure who wrote it. The language seems to intentionally refer to one who is both king and son. Most agree this is a messianic reference, foreshadowing Jesus Christ.

Now compare the psalm to the lyrics of this Christmas song:

> Hail to the Lord's Anointed,
> Great David's greater Son!
> Hail in the time appointed,
> His reign on earth begun!

Both psalm and song refer to the Anointed One, son and king, the Messiah himself, Jesus Christ.

Preparing for Christmas

There is a sense that the name *Jesus* is a personal reference, while *Christ* is a more transcendent reference to the Messiah. How do you respond to each name of Jesus Christ? How is he Jesus to you? How is he Christ to you?

> *Lord God, during this season of Christmas, I ask*
> *that you would focus me on the full significance*
> *of Jesus Christ, both Son of Man and Son of*
> *God, the Messiah, the Anointed One.*

The term *Xmas* is not about taking Christ out of Christmas. In fact, quite the opposite.

Ace Collins explains, "Many of the Gentiles who became the initial followers of Christ were Greek. The Greek for Christ's name is *Xristos* (pronounced *Christos*). . . . Many Greeks also used the letter X

... as their symbol of faith. This *X* marked the places where they worshiped."[9] The *X* also was a symbol of the cross.

Over time, among people who could not read or write, the *X* was a recognizable symbol substituted for "Christ on the cross," a meaningful shorthand for their faith in the name of Jesus.

6
Magi

Magi from the east came to Jerusalem and asked, "Where is the one who has been born king of the Jews? We saw his star when it rose and have come to worship him."

MATTHEW 2:1–2

We see them throughout the Old Testament, hanging around the courts of kings. Wise men. Advisers. Magi. In Genesis, the Egyptian pharaoh has a strange dream and calls his "magicians and wise men" to interpret it (41:8). In Exodus, another pharaoh calls his "wise men and sorcerers" to duplicate the God-given miracles of Moses (7:11–12).

In Esther 1:13, King Xerxes of Persia consults "experts" and "wise men" to figure out how to handle his disobedient queen (Esther's predecessor). In the book of Daniel, the Babylonian king has a disturbing dream, which he forgets, and he demands to be told what he dreamt. His advisers protest, but only Daniel can do what the king wants. "No wise man, enchanter, magician or diviner can explain to the king the mystery he has asked about," the Hebrew prophet explains, "but there is a God in heaven who reveals mysteries" (2:27–28).

Various Hebrew words and Greek renderings are used for these roles. Among them is the Greek *magos*, from which we get the Latin plural *magi*. So when Matthew uses this term to describe

32

those who traveled from "the east" to bring gifts to the newborn king, we have some history. We don't know much about these particular wise ones, but we can make some good guesses.

It's quite possible that Matthew's magi were connected to a royal court. This might also explain why they had little trouble getting an audience with Herod. (It's interesting that he confers with his own "wise men" to learn where the child would be born.)

Popular knowledge of the magi is pretty much wrong—at least as impressed upon us by the Christmas carol "We Three Kings."

There is no reason to think that they themselves were kings. The "three kings" tradition developed later in church history, possibly with reference to certain Old Testament prophecies (see Psalms 68:29; 72:10; Isaiah 60:3).

And the only reason to think there were three of them is that they brought three gifts. There might have been two or five or seven magi who all chipped in on the presents. One early church leader suggested there were twelve, but that was a trendy number at the time.

They came from "the east," which allows for a number of possibilities. Persia had a tradition of magi in the priestly class of its Zoroastrian religion. Babylon had a long-standing reputation for stargazing and wisdom (going back to Daniel and beyond). Some scholars think the gifts came from Arabia, so maybe the magi did too. This was the "east" of the Jewish world at the time, not the East we think of now as China and Japan and Korea.

The biblical text mentions "the house" where the magi visited the child (Matthew 2:11). This challenges the common notion that magi were elbowing shepherds in the stable to get a look at the baby Jesus. In fact, the magi probably came later, maybe when

Jesus was a toddler. Herod's order to kill children two years old or younger suggests that the magi showed up one to two years after Jesus's birth.

So they weren't kings, there weren't necessarily three of them, they didn't come from the East as we know it, and they weren't huddled around the manger as we like to depict them in our crèche decorations at Christmas. So who *were* they?

Some translations call the magi "astrologers." It's not a bad description, since we know they were studying the stars, but we should keep in mind that in most ancient cultures religion and science were nearly identical. We might consider the magi astronomers who examined the skies for clues about divine forces.

There are many theories about what they saw up there, what made them think it was a royal birth announcement, and how the star led them to the Christ child. We won't get into all that, but clearly the magi were in the business of reading meaning in heavenly configurations.

Also, it's appropriate that God used a dream to dissuade the magi from returning to Herod. Dream interpretation was in the job description of most magi.

Remember also that Daniel issued some prophecies that involved specific timing—periods of years described as "weeks" (9:20–27 NKJV). We're not going to do the math here, but it's possible that the magi did the numbers and believed that the Anointed One described by Daniel would be born in Daniel's homeland *in their time*. So when they saw the heavenly sign, they knew—game on! Divine prophecies were being fulfilled.

They undertook a major journey with expensive gifts, based on their conviction that this was a very special event.

We might rightly ask the question, What's the spiritual meaning of the magi?

Consider what Matthew is up to.

In chapter 1, he acknowledges that Jesus is born out of wedlock. It takes a dream from God to convince Joseph to stay with Mary. Before that, Matthew goes through one branch of Jesus's family tree, including only four women—two foreigners and two marked by scandal.

And here in chapter 2, the Christ child is worshiped by foreign dignitaries who are guided by God but involved in divination, sorcery, and magic—all strongly forbidden in the Jewish law.

Clearly Matthew is not interested in showing how holy everyone is, and he's making a point to include these foreign magi. We might suppose that Matthew is making a point: God, remarkably, uses flawed people and outsiders in his plan to redeem the world.

William Chatterton Dix was an English poet and hymn writer. He penned the lyrics to the well-known carol "What Child Is This?" But he also wrote a lesser-known Christmas hymn, "As with Gladness Men of Old."

Notably, in this carol Dix avoided a number of the wise men myths, referring to them only as "men of old" and never stating how many there were.

The hymn is sung to the same familiar tune of "For the Beauty of the Earth." The fourth verse is especially poignant in linking us today to the star the magi followed:

> Holy Jesus, ev'ry day
> Keep us in the narrow way;

And, when earthly things are past,
Bring our ransomed souls at last
Where they need no star to guide,
Where no clouds thy glory hide.

Preparing for Christmas

The magi symbolize how the gift of Jesus Christ, salvation it-self, is open to everyone, even outsiders. In what areas of life are you an outsider? Where in your times at work and with family do you feel on the outside? Consider the amazing grace of God to include you in his salvation plan. Perhaps in this Christmas season when you think of the magi, you might think of yourself likewise as an outsider being beckoned to worship the Son.

Lord God of the stars and heavens, thank
you for leading me to the Christ child.
Thank you for including me in your family.

We like one particular theory about the magi, though we have to admit it's conjecture. More than five hundred years before Jesus's birth, the prophet Daniel so impressed the king of Babylon that he was placed "in charge of all its wise men" (Daniel 2:48). Presumably this included the enchanters, diviners, and magi mentioned earlier in that chapter. Is it possible that Daniel began a tradition of scientific and prophetic wisdom in the court of Babylon and later in the Medo-Persian court, and that a society of wise men passed on this tradition through many generations?

7

Gifts

On coming to the house, they saw the child with his mother Mary, and they bowed down and worshiped him. Then they opened their treasures and presented him with gifts of gold, frankincense and myrrh.

MATTHEW 2:11

The word *gifts* is the centerpiece of an interesting sentence in Matthew's account of the magi's adoration of the Christ child. The Greek word is *dora*, which carries some emphasis on the freedom of the giver. A gift is not a payment or a bribe but a free expression of love, or in this case worship. This word appears in Ephesians 2:8, describing salvation as a "gift of God," not earned by religious works. (By the way, a different word, *charismata*, is used for "*spiritual* gifts.")

Even more fittingly, we often see *dora* used for offerings brought to the temple. In the Sermon on the Mount, Jesus mentions a case of someone bringing a gift (*doron*) to the altar (Matthew 5:23). This might be a bird or animal or some grain or incense offered as a sacrifice on the altar. But in Jesus's time there were collection boxes positioned in the temple courtyard where people could also give money. The collection box was called a "treasury."

Word lovers will adore the fact that the Greek word for "treasury" is *thesauros*. Perhaps you have used a thesaurus (or a thesaurus command on your computer) to access a treasury of words with similar meanings. That's just the Latin spelling of the Greek word used for the collection box in the temple—or for the treasure chest from which the magi pulled out gold, frankincense, and myrrh.

That's right. They opened their *thesaurous* and presented Jesus with gifts. Maybe each gift had its own protective box; we don't know. But Matthew's language speaks volumes about what's going on in this scene. Normally people would come to the temple, God's house, and put gifts (*dora*) into the collection boxes (*thesaurous*) as part of their worship. Here the magi come to a house (2:11) to worship the Christ child. They present gifts (*dora*) from out of their treasure boxes (*thesaurous*).

The message: this child is the rightful recipient of people's offerings and worship.

The gifts were expensive.

Gold, as you know, was a precious metal, and still is—not something working-class people saw much of. Frankincense and myrrh were aromatic substances produced from the gum of specific trees. We find both these products mentioned in Song of Songs:

> Who is this sweeping in from the wilderness
>   like a cloud of smoke?
> Who is it, fragrant with myrrh and frankincense
>   and every kind of spice?
> Look, it is Solomon's carriage. (3:6–7 NLT)

Who but the wealthy king could afford to import myrrh and frankincense?

We might take a lesson from this. The gifts offered to the Christ child were fit for kings. These were the "house gifts" one brought to a royal court on regal occasions. The wise men probably expected to encounter a king on a throne, and they presented these expensive gifts.

David and Barbara Leeman make the connection to us today: "Christmas gifts remain a holiday custom, but at some point, our gifts changed from gifts to God into gifts to one another. Giving one another gifts at Christmas is not wrong. But the question should be asked, what are you giving to God in your Christmas worship?"[10]

One Christmas hymn beautifully answers this question. "Brightest and Best of the Stars of the Morning" recounts the wise men's gifts:

> Shall we yield Him in costly devotion
> Rarest of fragrances, tribute divine,
> Gems of the mountain and pearls of the ocean,
> Myrrh from the forest and gold from the mine?

But the hymn soon observes how inadequate those gifts are and comes to the understanding that "richer by far is the heart's adoration."

The only gift of real worth to God is ourselves.

Preparing for Christmas

Remember that God's whole plan for our salvation is for the purpose of being close to us. He desires communion with you. So think about this: in this Christmas season, your gift to God might just be your presence, some time spent with God each day. Maybe, just maybe, you could put that under the tree.

Lord, this Christmas I offer to you the only gift I have that's of value to you—myself. I wish to spend time with you, in conversation and communion, each day.

Some scholars note that Arabia is home to the trees that produce frankincense and myrrh, and thus the magi must have come from there. Maybe, but trade was common in the ancient world. Even in Babylon or Persia, the magi would have had access to traders, importing all sorts of treasures from all sorts of places. Frankincense and myrrh were expensive, like gold, but that was appropriate for a newborn king. Still, the Arabian theory would make the magi an obvious fulfillment of Isaiah 60:6: "The people of Sheba [in Arabia] will bring gold and frankincense and will come worshiping the LORD" (NLT).

8

Joy

But the angel reassured them. "Don't be afraid!"
he said. "I bring you good news that will bring
great joy to all people."

LUKE 2:10 NLT

In *The Lion, the Witch and the Wardrobe*, C. S. Lewis's classic fairy-tale allegory, young Lucy Pevensie encounters a place that's frozen and snow covered. She learns from Mr. Tumnus the faun that the land of Narnia was once verdantly green and beautiful. He tells her that the White Witch has cast a spell over it. Here, he says, it's "always winter and never Christmas."[11]

In the first paragraph, we learn that the children were sent away from London "because of the air-raids," setting Lewis's story against the backdrop of World War II during the bombing of England. But there's a larger context for Narnia, which is, of course, nothing less than the story of God and humankind and the winter of sin we live in.

In order to talk about the joy of Christmas, we must understand this larger context of God, Jesus, and us. The joy of the holidays is not the empty, forced glitz of shopping malls and the sticky sweetness of candy canes. The joy of Christmas is found in the sobering reality of a world where "it's always winter." Into this world a Savior is born, coming to conquer the deep freeze of our sin.

Jesus Christ brings to us a new dawn, not just for a day but for all of time. *This* is the real joy of Christmas.

As we see the word *joy* throughout Scripture, it indicates both a feeling and an expression. In fact, it's hard to imagine having joy without showing it. The Bible shows people singing for joy, shouting for joy, and even leaping for joy. King David dances. Farm workers carry sheaves of produce, singing. A woman finds her lost coin and calls her neighbors to rejoice with her. And the shepherds rush to see the Christ child and then spread the word about him.

Early Greek philosophers connected joy (*chara*) with pleasure (*hedone*). Some liked pleasure, others not so much. Hedonistic Epicureans have long been associated with the catchphrase "eat, drink, and be merry, for tomorrow we die" (see Luke 12:19). On the other hand, the Stoics distrusted all human passions, but some carved out a place for "good moods" like joy. *Chaire* became a common greeting in Greek derived from the word for "joy." When the angel announces the coming birth of Jesus to Mary, he says, "*Chaire*, you who are highly favored!" (1:28).

The Hebrew concept of joy was much more, shall we say, organic. Here's where we find all the singing, shouting, and leaping. The source of that joy is the Lord himself. "In Your presence is fullness of joy," sings the psalmist, "at Your right hand are pleasures forevermore" (Psalm 16:11 NKJV).

Because of this, we "worship the LORD with gladness" and "come before him with joyful songs" (100:2). While worship may include contemplation, repentance, and sacrifice, it is commonly associated with joy.

The Lord also rejoices. We see glimpses of this in the creation account in Genesis 1, where the work on each day is proclaimed "good" and on the last day "very good." This is a Creator who loves creating. "I will create Jerusalem to be a delight and its people a joy," he says through the prophet Isaiah. "I will rejoice over Jerusalem and take delight in my people" (65:18–19).

He especially finds joy in his relationship with his people: "As a bridegroom rejoices over his bride, so will your God rejoice over you" (62:5). The prophets anticipate a future time when that relationship will be restored. "He will take great delight in you; in his love he will no longer rebuke you, but will rejoice over you with singing" (Zephaniah 3:17).

The joyful announcement of the angel suggests that Christmas is the beginning of the fulfillment of these prophecies, the patching up of this relationship. "Rejoice greatly, Daughter Zion!" says Zechariah. "Shout, Daughter Jerusalem! See, your king comes to you" (9:9). That is, of course, a Palm Sunday prophecy, but it was thirty years earlier that the fulfillment began in a manger in Bethlehem.

And so we come to the new dawn, the birth of Jesus Christ.

The angel tells the shepherds, "I bring you good news that will bring great joy to all people" (Luke 2:10 NLT). As with all Scripture passages, translators have to make some interpretive choices here. Literally, the Greek says, "I evangelize to you great joy, which will be to all the people." The verb *euangelizomai* already carries the meaning "I announce good news," but "great joy" is the direct object.

Fascinating, isn't it, that the birth announcement of the Messiah focuses on joy. The angel could have told the shepherds about the theology of salvation, the history of God's dealings with Israel, or the moral responsibilities on those who would worship this child—but no. The headline on heaven's website is JOY.

The joy of Christmas is not based on good fortune, happy experiences, or pleasure. It is not the season to be *jolly* in the superficial way so often presented. The joy of Christmas is our joy in Jesus and the amazing wonder that he has come to save us.

Preparing for Christmas

How might your life still be frozen in sin? What is your current winter? Perhaps you know Jesus as your Savior but have grown away from him and find yourself out in the cold once again. Make this Christmas a time to recover your relationship with him. Confess your sins and clothe yourself in his saving warmth. Step back into the joy of Jesus, and make him the Lord of your story.

Father God, help me engage this Christmas in the truth
of its meaning. I want to recover the faith I once had.
Lead me into the fuller joy of Jesus this season.

The Christmas carol about joy that's most familiar is, of course, "Joy to the World." Nothing quite matches its exuberance.

But another hymn captures the joy of Jesus's birth in the larger context of time: "Joy Has Dawned (Across the World)." Look it up. In four short stanzas, the hymn walks us through the Christmas story, concluding in a crescendoed "Once a babe in Bethlehem, now the Lord of history."[12]

9

Herod

When Herod realized that he had been outwitted by the Magi, he was furious.

MATTHEW 2:16

At the heart of the Christmas account of Jesus's birth lies an espionage story. Not James Bond exactly, though its antagonist, Herod, might be an earlier version of Dr. No.

Of course, the biblical account reports that King Herod called for a private executive meeting with the wise men. Herod cleverly told them, "Go and search carefully for the child. As soon as you find him, report to me, so that I too may go and worship him" (Matthew 2:8).

The Bible tells us that the wise men did indeed find the boy Jesus, worshiped him, and gave him gifts. But they were then warned in a dream *not* to return to Herod as he had instructed. Secretly they returned home the back way.

Herod realized he'd been outwitted by the Magi, and he was not a happy camper. He ordered the slaughter of all the boys in Bethlehem two years and under.

Meanwhile (back at the ranch), Joseph and Mary had been warned in a dream to escape, and they took the child Jesus to Egypt to avoid the cruel violence of King Herod.

Wow—such dramatic suspense with the evil Herod at the heart of it. So what do we know about Dr. No—ah, this King

Herod, who tried through trickery to snuff out Jesus, this "pretender" king and threat to his throne?

In Shakespeare's classic play *Hamlet*, the Danish prince coaches a group of actors, warning them not to overact. "It out-Herods Herod. Pray you, avoid it."[13]

He was probably referring to Christmas pageants of that time, in which the role of Herod was played bombastically and flamboyantly in flourishes of overacting. Historically, though, the real Herod seems more like a conniver, cleverly plotting to gain and keep power.

Herod came to power as a young man in the 40s BC. His father was a respected general who gained influence by backing the right horses in the civil strife that consumed Palestine for decades. One of those "horses" was Rome, whose armies conquered Jerusalem in 63 BC but still faced internal conflict back home.

As a young governor in Galilee, Herod showed skill in putting down rebellions, but invaders from the east forced him to flee . . . to Rome, where he made the acquaintance of a young man about his own age named Octavian, who soon took power as Augustus Caesar.

It's good to have friends in high places. Octavian had Herod appointed king of Judea in 40 BC. Herod was about twenty-five years old when he returned to rule his homeland with the mighty support of Rome.

Except it wasn't really his homeland. As influential as they were, Herod's family came from Idumea (old Edom), across the Jordan River. Enemies often depicted Herod as a usurper, a pretender, not fully Jewish. Some thought the magnificent temple he built in Jerusalem was a bribe to quiet his religious enemies.

And it was a magnificent temple. It out-Solomoned Solomon. The building project was so massive that it was still in progress half a century after Herod died. Herod launched other building projects as well. A racetrack and theater in Jerusalem helped make it a Greek-style city. He built fortresses in the wilderness and cities on the sea.

He seemed increasingly paranoid as he grew older, and not without reason. He now had a number of heirs, each one with personal ambitions. He was also getting sick. So when the magi asked about a newborn king of the Jews, it must have set off all sorts of alarms. For decades, Herod had used violence to guard his power. What was this new threat?

We see his conniving spirit in his pleasant request to the magi to report back to him. We see his murderous intent in the order to kill the babies of Bethlehem.

Herods are a bit like cockroaches. One dies and another three crawl out.

King Herod the Great, who met with the magi, was the first of a royal line that included others who interacted with the adult Jesus, John the Baptist, Peter, and Paul. All in all, they were an unsavory lot.

While hiding out in Egypt, Joseph and Mary got word of the death of Herod the Great. Taking the throne of Judea was his son Herod Archelaus, who was just as dangerous, so the holy family resettled in Galilee, where Herod Antipas ruled (Matthew 2:22).

Archelaus was such a terrible king that *Jews and Samaritans teamed up* to beg Rome to remove him. A Roman governor was appointed over Judea, replacing him. Meanwhile, Herod Antipas reigned in Galilee for several decades. This was the Herod who had John the Baptist beheaded and interviewed Jesus before his crucifixion.

This family of Herods continues through the New Testament. Rome set up Herod Agrippa I, grandson of Herod the Great, as king over the territory of Antipas. Agrippa was the Herod who executed James, the brother of John, and imprisoned Peter. His son, Herod Agrippa II, was called in by a Roman governor to confer with Paul, who shared the good news of Jesus. Agrippa II famously scoffed, "Do you think that in such a short time you can persuade me to be a Christian?" (Acts 26:28).

What's our takeaway from this lineage of Herod kings?

Perhaps, during this Christmas season of delight and exuberant joy, we might be soberly reminded of this threat to the baby Jesus. We might look in awe at our God who directed an ingenious counterplot that involved wise men in the court of Herod, a vivid dream, and a secret getaway.

If it weren't true, it would make a great espionage novel.

Preparing for Christmas

In your devotional time, take a moment to listen to a version of the sixteenth-century "Coventry Carol." It's a haunting tune set in a minor key that captures the foreboding of Herod's plot against the baby Jesus:

> Herod the king, in his raging,
> Charged he hath this day
> His men of might, in his own sight
> All young children to slay.

An ominous song, for sure, against the backdrop of a joyful season, but maybe there's a useful lesson in it for us. Maybe we should be aware that there's always a Herod in our lives—someone who tries to snuff out our faith. The Enemy is looking for every possible angle to worm into our minds and hearts to kill our relationship with God.

What are those threats to your Christ-life right now?

Lord God, I bring to you the Herods of my life, the evils that threaten my faith. Give me your wisdom to escape from them. I need your power to overcome them.

10

Peace

And he will be called Wonderful Counselor, Mighty God,
Everlasting Father, Prince of Peace.

ISAIAH 9:6

After one angel announced the birth of Jesus to the shepherds, a whole choir of angels burst into song. "Glory to God in the highest heaven," they sang, "and on earth peace . . ." (Luke 2:14).

At that point the sound kicked out.

No, not really, but there are disagreements about how to translate the rest of that sentence. Literally, they said, "On earth peace to people good pleasure." This is in a poetic form, so the word order doesn't help much. Four hundred years ago, the King James Version translators took one approach—"good will to men"—and that has become embedded in the Christmas story.

But recent scholars have reexamined the verse, suggesting that it should be "people of good pleasure." Clearly it is talking about God's good pleasure. So the New International Version has "peace to those on whom his favor rests." Most other modern translations follow suit.

Any way you read it, peace is at the heart of the song. This is a huge word in the Scriptures, a major theme in both Testaments.

The Hebrew word for "peace" is *shalom*. You may recognize that as a Jewish greeting. This goes back to biblical times. Some of the "How are you?" greetings in the Bible are literally "Is there peace with you?" (2 Samuel 20:9; see also Genesis 43:27). Peace has the sense of well-being, health, everything being all right.

We can learn more about peace from its opposites. "Too long have I lived among those who hate peace," a psalmist complains. "I am for peace; but when I speak, they are for war" (Psalm 120:6–7). In the war-torn world of the ancient Middle East, a lengthy reign without conflict was worth noting (2 Chronicles 14:1, 5–6).

Conflict isn't always about armies. Discord arises within families and communities. "Even my close friend, someone I trusted, one who shared my bread, has turned against me," another psalmist moans (Psalm 41:9). His term for "close friend" is *ish shalom*, "man of my peace."

This is probably the kind of problem Jesus had in mind when he said, "Blessed are the peacemakers" (Matthew 5:9). He often talked about forgiving others, being reconciled to other parties in a dispute, and even loving your enemies.

Sometimes peace is the opposite of anxiety or fear. "In peace I will lie down and sleep," says a psalm of David, "for you alone, LORD, make me dwell in safety" (Psalm 4:8).

"Peace I leave with you," Jesus told his disciples, "my peace I give you. I do not give to you as the world gives. Do not let your hearts be troubled and do not be afraid" (John 14:27). How does the peace of Jesus differ from the world's peace? Perhaps it's not about avoiding hardship but about growing through it. Maybe it's more than "Don't worry, be happy," and instead "I am trusting the Lord."

Paul urged the Philippians to avoid anxiety by praying. "In every situation, by prayer and petition, with thanksgiving, present your requests to God. And the peace of God, which transcends all understanding, will guard your hearts and your minds in Christ Jesus" (4:6–7).

So, when the angels sang about "peace on earth," what kind of peace were they talking about? When God said to Ezekiel, "I will make a covenant of peace with them" (37:26), what did he mean? When Paul writes, "Therefore, since we have been justified through faith, we have peace with God through our Lord Jesus Christ" (Romans 5:1), what "peace" does he refer to?

Surely the angels were announcing that the babe in the manger was a peace offering from God to humanity. The glorious God in heaven was showing his good pleasure to people by sending his Son.

The Ezekiel passage tells us that peace isn't a single flash in the night but a long-term agreement: "It will be an everlasting covenant. . . . My dwelling place will be with them; I will be their God, and they will be my people" (37:26–27).

The apostle Paul, in talking about justification through faith, is alluding to a communion with God that wasn't before possible. By his own sacrifice, the Prince of Peace tore down the wall of sin separating a holy God from a sinful humanity. We can be at peace, relationally, with God.

Paul would go on to say that God intends peace to be our own relational practice with each other: Because the Spirit of Christ lives within us, we exhibit love, joy, peace, and patience in our everyday lives (Galatians 5:22–23). Interpersonal conflicts arise, but we "make every effort to do what leads to peace and to mutual edification" (Romans 14:19).

The advent of Christ is a promise of peace in all these ways— peace on earth, justification with God, personal peace with friends and family. We rightly rejoice in this, yet we're aware Christmas is kind of a silent-night-time-out from the discord and violence of the world. In a matter of days, we must return to the noise and dissonance of life. So, the Christmas season is bittersweet as we realize real peace is partial, not yet complete.

Jesus himself told us this: "These things I have spoken to you, that in Me you may have peace. In the world you will have tribulation; but be of good cheer, I have overcome the world" (John 16:33 NKJV).

We have peace, right here and now, in Jesus, the Prince of Peace. Yet much peace is yet to come.

The Christmas carol favorite "Silent Night" is usually sung in the bright key of C major. But some have put it in a minor key, giving it a plaintive, yearning quality. Perhaps the minor key is actually more appropriate for the song's wishful refrain, "sleep in heavenly peace."

There is in the promise of peace at Christmastime a minor key. We are painfully aware of how difficult peace is to achieve in a world at war, among relationships at odds, inside our own anxious and worried hearts. The peace we embrace at Christmas is an ideal, a poignant hope that someday we might experience true and full well-being. We rejoice in the promise of peace that Christ brings, though we know that peace is not here now. Not yet.

Preparing for Christmas

Consider those areas of your life that are stressful, that make you anxious, that bring you conflict. Perhaps you are in the middle of a difficult conflict with another person right now. What are those places of anxiety within you this Christmas season?

Bring them to God. Lay them at his feet. Absorb the words of the psalmist: "In peace I will lie down and sleep, for you alone, O LORD, will keep me safe" (Psalm 4:8 NLT). Allow the Prince of Peace to whisper to you.

O God, comfort my soul, ease my worries, bring me right now into your heavenly peace.

The custom of hanging mistletoe dates back to the first and second centuries. Over time, it became a symbol of peace. One writer reports that "Scandinavian warriors would stop fierce battles if they or the opposing soldiers suddenly found themselves under trees where mistletoe grew. They believed that to continue a war beneath the plant that God had given the world as a sign of life would dishonor him. A host of other societies soon adopted this rule as well. For millions of people, mistletoe became not just a symbol of peace, but a sign that demanded peace."[14]

11

Immanuel

*"The virgin will conceive and give birth to
a son, and they will call him Immanuel"
(which means "God with us").*

MATTHEW 1:23

Who can forget George Herman Ruth?

You might know him better by his nickname. "Babe" Ruth was one of the greatest baseball players of all time. Sportswriters called him "The Great Bambino" and "The Sultan of Swat."

One person can have a lot of names.

We find that in the Bible too, where names often carry important meanings. Prophets used names to convey divine messages. We can only wonder if Hosea's daughter carried any emotional scars from being named "Unloved," but God was delivering a stern message to the nation of Israel. Later God says, "I will show love to those I called 'Not loved'" (Hosea 2:23 NLT).

Isaiah predicted the birth of a child whose "name will be called Wonderful, Counselor, Mighty God, Everlasting Father, Prince of Peace" (Isaiah 9:6 NKJV). Though this prophecy was clearly fulfilled in Jesus, it's doubtful that Mary ever called him in for dinner saying, "Hey, Prince of Peace, come and get it!"

Yet each of those names gives us a message about his identity.

The same is true for a Hebrew name we encounter two chapters earlier in Isaiah: Immanuel. It's a message more than a moniker. And at the time, King Ahaz desperately needed to get that message. Immanuel means "God with us."

Spiritually, King Ahaz was a mess. 2 Kings 16 and 2 Chronicles 28 tell his story, from somewhat different perspectives. Isaiah 7 gives us a third view. Though his father and grandfather had ruled the nation of Judah in ways that generally pleased the Lord, Ahaz did not. He was enamored with the gods of other cultures. On a trip to Damascus, he saw a pagan altar he liked and had one made just like it for the temple in Jerusalem. He promoted pagan religious practices throughout Judah, almost as if he was trying to keep all the gods happy.

Politically, King Ahaz carried on an extended conflict with two neighboring nations, Israel (the northern kingdom, also known as Ephraim or Samaria) and Aram (Syria). When those two countries joined together to fight Judah, Ahaz made a foolish alliance with the superpower Assyria, far to the east, inviting that army to come and knock off these two minor nuisances.

That's when Isaiah showed up with a prophecy about a baby being born. While we recognize the major fulfillment of this prophecy seven centuries later in Bethlehem, it also had an immediate aspect. A young woman—some scholars think she was Isaiah's wife, or perhaps someone in the court of Ahaz—would have a baby. Before that child knew right from wrong (poetically Isaiah is describing a time period of maybe five to seven years), the threats from the neighbor nations would vanish.

The child's name: Immanuel. God with us.

The name delivered to Ahaz a strong message: *So, Ahaz, you don't need to sacrifice to every deity that catches your fancy. The one true God is here, with you, and cares about what you're doing. If you let him, God will prove himself to you. But you insist on finding your own way.*

If you had to boil down the Bible to one sentence, this is a pretty good one: God is with us. The Old Testament shows the Lord interacting with his people in a multitude of ways, and in the New Testament we see Immanuel himself, Jesus Christ, taking on human flesh and living among human beings.

In the Psalms and some of the prophets, we occasionally hear cries of doubt: "Where are you when I need you, Lord?" (see Psalms 42:3; 115:2). But turn the page and you're likely to find a reminder that God is with us, "an ever-present help in trouble" (46:1). Even in the darkest valleys, we can "fear no evil, for you are with me" (23:4). When we're tempted to think, "My cause is disregarded by my God" (Isaiah 40:27), we receive the assurance, "Do not fear, for I am with you" (41:10).

Not only did Jesus promise his disciples, "I am with you always" (Matthew 28:20), but he also promised to send the Holy Spirit to live in us (John 14:17). Suddenly, God's presence is not just *with* us but *in* us. This is the world-changing mystery that Paul proclaimed: "Christ in you, the hope of glory" (Colossians 1:27).

And in the glorious scene at the end of the Bible, a voice from heaven announces, "Look! God's dwelling place is now among the people, and he will dwell with them. They will be his people, and God himself will be with them and be their God" (Revelation 21:3).

Preparing for Christmas

The Christmas carol "O Come, O Come, Emmanuel" is a song that recounts some of the names of Jesus. It's a mournful tune with a hopeful message. Like one of the psalms of lament, it bemoans Israel's long wait for the Messiah: "O come . . . and ransom captive Israel that mourns in lonely exile here until the Son of God appear."

The carol is usually sung in the key of E minor, which fits its plaintive verses but seems at odds with its jubilant chorus: "Rejoice! Rejoice! Immanuel shall come to you, O Israel." Rejoicing here becomes a kind of melancholic hope.

John Piper well articulates the unique beauty of this carol: "Sorrows touch every Christian. . . . It is a wonderful thing that there are Christmas carols that are written for the real world of sorrowful joy, as well as the real world of exuberant joy. 'O Come, O Come, Emmanuel' is one of them."[15]

You might look up the lyrics for "O Come, O Come, Emmanuel." Each of the verses includes a name or phrase describing the Messiah—"Lord of might," "Branch of Jesse," "Key of David," and so on. Use each verse to worship the Lord of your life.

Lord Immanuel, I know you are "God with me," but I ask that you come close to me in these moments, in this season. I think of the names for you used in verse and song, and ponder all that you are to me and others. Thank you for what you've done in my life.

Both *Immanuel* and *Emmanuel* are found in the Bible and mean the same thing. *Immanuel* is generally found in the Old Testament and *Emmanuel* in the New Testament, although modern translations tend to normalize the spelling in both Old Testament and New Testament as *Immanuel*. The variation of spelling is simply due to the differences between Hebrew (Old Testament) and Greek (New Testament).

12

Jesus

And he gave him the name Jesus.

MATTHEW 1:25

Within five verses in Matthew's account, the naming of the Christ child is mentioned three separate times: "You are to give him the name Jesus," "They will call him Immanuel," and "He gave him the name Jesus" (1:21, 23, 25).

Hmm, must be something important in the name thing.

Jesus is the English form of the Greek name *Iesous* that is the counterpart for the Hebrew name *Yehoshua* (or sometimes *Yeshua*), which is brought back into English as *Joshua*.

Got that?

In Hebrew, the name means "Yahweh is salvation," or perhaps "God saves."

Joseph was told to give Mary's child this name "because he will save his people from their sins" (Matthew 1:21).

And this was the name he was known by throughout his earthly ministry. He was "Jesus of Nazareth" or "Jesus the carpenter's son." His disciples generally called him "Lord" or "Rabbi." The full name "Jesus Christ" was a bold statement calling him the promised Messiah. This came into use among his followers later.

The popularity of names changes from season to season. In America, the most popular baby boy name currently is Liam. In France, the most common male name is Gabriel; among Spanish newborns, the most common boy name is Santiago.

In ancient times, Yeshua/Iesous/Jesus was not an unusual name. The Bible mentions several other people who share it. Paul sends greetings to the Colossians from a Jesus Justus. In the Old Testament, there are several Joshuas, including two who emerge as interesting prefigurements of Christ—if you want to see them that way.

The most prominent was the successor of Moses as leader of the Israelites. Joshua son of Nun appears early in the Bible as an aide to Moses and as a scout who urges the Israelites to trust God and invade Canaan. Later, as the nation's new leader, he spearheads the conquest of Israel's once and future homeland. Not just a military leader, Joshua issued a memorable spiritual challenge as well: "Choose for yourselves this day whom you will serve. . . . But as for me and my household, we will serve the LORD" (Joshua 24:15).

Another Joshua emerged after the Babylonian captivity, as the Jews were resettling Judea. He served as high priest, with Zerubbabel as the nation's political leader. The prophet Zechariah had strange visions about him: "'Listen, High Priest Joshua, you and your associates seated before you, who are men symbolic of things to come: I am going to bring my servant, the Branch. See, the stone I have set in front of Joshua! There are seven eyes on that one stone, and I will engrave an inscription on it,' says the LORD Almighty, 'and I will remove the sin of this land in a single day'" (Zechariah 3:8–9).

Was it a coincidence that the high priest—"symbolic of things to come"—shared the name of the Son of God who would actually remove humanity's sin in a single day? Not likely.

Names are important in Scripture. Names of God are especially important. People then and now have tried to harness the supernatural power of the divine name, but Scripture keeps calling us into a relationship with the Name Bearer. Is there power in the name of Jesus? Yes, but not because of the way the vowels and consonants slide off the tongue. The power comes from Jesus's love for us, his sacrifice, his promise of redemption. That's why we look forward to the time when

> at the name of Jesus every knee should bow,
>> in heaven and on earth and under the earth,
> and every tongue acknowledge that Jesus Christ is Lord,
>> to the glory of God the Father. (Philippians 2:10–11)

"At the Name of Jesus" is a hymn penned by an English poet with a very appropriate seasonal name—Caroline Maria Noel. She wrote poems for her own meditational use that were especially personal to her because she suffered much of her life from chronic illness and pain. She eventually published a volume of her poetry under the title *The Name of Jesus, and Other Verses, for the Sick and Lonely.*

This hymn is not strictly known as a Christmas carol, being more often associated with Ascension Day. However, it fits so well in our holiday singing, precisely because Christmas was so very much about the naming of the newborn Christ, Jesus.

Preparing for Christmas

The fifth verse of "At the Name of Jesus" goes like this:

> In your hearts enthrone Him; there let Him subdue
> All that is not holy, all that is not true;
> Crown Him as your Captain in temptation's hour;
> Let His will enfold you in its light and power.

Take a few moments to read yourself into those words. What does the name of Jesus mean to you? Maybe the better question is whether the name of Jesus really makes a difference in your life. As this hymn so rightly puts it, the name of Jesus means he is to be enthroned in our hearts and subdue "all that is not holy" and true in our lives. Does the name of Jesus make that kind of difference in your daily life? Are you willing for Jesus to "subdue" that within you which is not "holy and true"? What do you need to turn over to him to make him truly the captain of your life?

Lord Jesus, I come to you humbly with certain areas of my life that I need to turn over to you. Take ownership of that in me which is not true.

"There are two hundred and fifty-six names given in the Bible for the Lord Jesus Christ, and I suppose this was because He was infinitely beyond all that any one name could express." —Billy Sunday[16]

13

Star

The star they had seen when it rose went ahead of them until it stopped over the place where the child was. When they saw the star, they were overjoyed.

MATTHEW 2:9-10

It makes sense that wise stargazers, who attached meaning to every part of the night sky, might receive a message from God in that way.

Many scholars think the star followed by the magi was actually a conjunction of planets that appeared within a constellation that was associated with the Jews. As astronomers trace the movements of stars and planets backward through time (yes, they can do that), there are a few heavenly events like that in the time around Jesus's birth.

On several other occasions in ancient history, it was claimed that astronomical signs predicted or celebrated royal births. So we can see how an unusual brightness in the Jewish part of the sky might send the magi to the palace in Jerusalem. Surely that was where a new king of the Jews would be born. The surprise comes when the star continues to serve as divine GPS. "The star they had seen when it rose went ahead of them until it stopped over the place where the child was" (Matthew 2:9).

How would this happen? A star (or planet) is millions of miles away—how do you know what landmark it's "over"? Questions abound as we look for explanations in the natural world, but this was a supernatural event. Was this perhaps an angel? Angels are often described as "shining" (Acts 10:30). Or remember the bright cloud that led the Israelites through the wilderness (Exodus 14:19–20)?

The details are puzzling, but somehow God led these "star students" on a very specific path, using something they interpreted as the same star that had started this whole journey.

The Greek word for "star" is *aster*, essentially the same as its Latin counterpart. We get *astronomy* from this root. The main Hebrew word is *kokab*, but on a few occasions the collection of heavenly stars is called *saba*, a term most often used for an army. You might have encountered this word in its plural form, *sabaoth*, describing the Lord of hosts, or Lord of armies. The concept takes a poetic form in Isaiah 40:26 (NLT):

> Look up into the heavens.
>   Who created all the stars?
> He brings them out like an army, one after another,
>   calling each by its name.

The ancient world didn't know what modern astronomers know about the nature of stars. They didn't know our sun is a star. But they did see the movements of the stars, and they grouped them in constellations. Various cultures saw the night sky as a canvas on which the images of their gods and heroes were drawn. The hunter Orion, with three strong stars on his belt and several other prominent stars that suggest the outline of a tall man, is one of these mythic figures. He comes from Greek mythology, but several other cultures have similar legends about this constellation as a strong hero who now lives in the night sky. The Hebrews had a different name for that constellation (*Kesil*, "fool") and a different story—about a big oaf who got himself tangled in a chain. In Job 38:31 in the Good News Translation, God asks, "Can you . . . loosen the bonds that hold Orion [*Kesil*]?" (see also Job 9:9; Amos 5:8).[17]

While the starry sky evoked stories about the gods of different lands, the repeated message of Scripture is strong: our God, the Creator, made all these stars.

"You have set your glory in the heavens," the psalmist muses, as he considers "the work of your fingers, the moon and the stars, which you have set in place" (Psalm 8:1, 3). Elsewhere, we're told, "He determines the number of the stars and calls them each by name" (147:4).

So why would you worship the stars instead of the God who "decrees the moon and stars to shine by night" (Jeremiah 31:35)? Yet this was a problem among the ancient Israelites. Deuteronomy warned about it. "And when you look up to the sky and see the sun, the moon and the stars—all the heavenly array—do not be enticed into bowing down to them and worshiping things the Lord your God has apportioned to all the nations under heaven" (4:19).

Apparently, though, star worship was happening—and we're not talking about the latest pop singer. Manasseh, son and successor of the great king Hezekiah, "bowed down to all the starry hosts and worshiped them. . . . In the two courts of the temple of the Lord, he built altars to all the starry hosts" (2 Kings 21:3, 5; see also Amos 5:26).

The ancients also looked to the stars for messages from distant deities. The Babylonians specialized in it, building observatories and charting constellations. They were quite proud of this merger of science and religion. And for a time they ruled their world.

But Isaiah, like other biblical prophets, warned of their downfall. Stargazing could only take you so far when you went up against the Creator of those stars.

> All the counsel you have received has only worn
>   you out!
>   Let your astrologers come forward,
> those stargazers who make predictions month by
>   month,
>   let them save you from what is coming upon
>   you. . . .
> They cannot even save themselves
>   from the power of the flame. (Isaiah 47:13–14)

There's an irony here. More than half a millennium after Isaiah wrote that, the magi—who may have been Babylonian astrologers themselves—were still looking to the stars for divine messages. And in the gracious plan of the creator God, they got one—the birth star that guided them to the Savior.

The carol "We Three Kings" may get the facts about the wise men wrong, but the refrain gets something right:

> O star of wonder, star of light,
> Star with royal beauty bright,
> Westward leading, still proceeding,
> Guide us to thy perfect light.

Quite simply, the Christmas star is depicted here not as the end itself but as that which guides us to the ultimate object of our worship. It guides us to the "perfect light," God himself.

Preparing for Christmas

This biblical history of celestial stars speaks to us in a personal way. In what areas of our lives do we substitute a sign or wonder or symbol as an object to be worshiped? Is our wonder for the symbol or for the God who created it?

Do we substitute Bible knowledge for our heart-faith in God? Is our charitable giving a pseudo alternate for giving *ourselves* to God? Do we make church into a stand-in for our relationship with God?

Father God, show me the ways in which I've worshiped a "star" instead of you.

In some cultures, the poinsettia plant is thought to represent the life of Jesus. The shape of its flowers and leaves symbolizes the Christmas star, its red leaves symbolize Jesus's shed blood on the cross, and its white leaves symbolize Christ's purity.

14
Shepherds

And there were shepherds living out in the fields nearby,
keeping watch over their flocks at night.

LUKE 2:8

Of course, the burning question at the heart of the Christmas story is not the astronomical origin of the Christmas star or the possibility of the virgin birth. It's why in the world were the shepherds tending their flocks in the middle of the night? Didn't they have other things to do? When did they rest?

To understand this, we need to take a deep dive into the business of sheep.

Sheep played a critical role in the economy of ancient Israel. Mutton was kosher, so they provided a good food source. Their wool could be woven into sturdy fabric. Sheepshearing parties brought communities together. And, hey—organic lawn mowing.

We sometimes look down on the shepherds of the Christmas story as menial laborers, dealing daily with the smell and mess of obstinate animals. While it's true that God often chooses "the lowly things of this world" (1 Corinthians 1:28), shepherds weren't considered that lowly in their own time. They were managers of business operations, responsible for significant economic resources. If a lamb wandered off, some profit went with it. So it was important to get good shepherds who would care diligently for their flocks, even if that meant running after the one out of a hundred that fled the fold (see Luke 15:3–7).

Sheep were also important in Israel's worship, used in temple sacrifices. This was especially true at Passover time each spring, when the temple staff worked overtime sacrificing lambs in accordance with the law, and when families generally had lamb as part of their sacred meal.

This gives us an important clue about the timing of that first Christmas—and an answer to our burning question.

Why were the shepherds tending their flocks by night? It's likely that they were working pre-Passover overtime. They would plan all year for Passover, a boom time for the sheep industry, especially in the vicinity of Jerusalem. Bethlehem was only five miles south, with lots of good pasture, so flocks might be gathered there in advance of the big day at the temple. It makes sense that shepherds would lead flocks out for feeding at different times of the day *and* night.

Passover would be a very appropriate time for the Lamb of God to enter our world (John 1:29). Sorry if that spoils your "Winter Wonderland" theme, but the first Christmas was probably in the spring. There's nothing in the Bible associating Christmas with winter, or with December 25. That connection came centuries later, in a fusion with a pagan holiday.

The biblical nativity story raises another question: What happened to the sheep?

The shepherds encountered the angel, and the angel choir, and rushed into town. Given the excitement of the moment, it might seem perfectly understandable if they left their sheep behind—but not if they were good shepherds.

The alternative paints a far more interesting picture—shepherds driving their fattened flocks into town with them and paying homage to the newborn king with the sound of baaing behind them.

Of course, it was no coincidence that shepherds were beckoned to the birth site.

The prophets had precisely predicted the birth of a shepherd-king:

> But you, Bethlehem Ephrathah . . .
> out of you will come for me
> one who will be ruler over Israel. . . .
>
> Therefore Israel will be abandoned
> until the time when she who is in labor bears a
> son. . . .
>
> He will stand and shepherd his flock
> in the strength of the LORD. (Micah 5:2–4)

Jesus identified himself as the Good Shepherd: "I know my sheep and my sheep know me" (John 10:14). Revelation calls Jesus the "Lord of lords and King of kings" (17:14).

Jesus, shepherd and king, was worshiped at his birth by shepherds and kings.

Preparing for Christmas

A more contemporary Christmas carol, "Where Shepherds Lately Knelt," personalizes the shepherds' experience at the birth of Christ. A modern-day seeker is the first-person narrator of the lyrics, coming to Jesus as the shepherds once did. In gorgeous poetry, the seeker expresses the wonder of Christmas: "Can I, will I forget how Love was born and burned its way into my heart . . . ?"[18]

As you stand beside the manger today, where is your heart? What is your need? Have you forgotten "how Love was born?" Do you need to remind yourself that Jesus is the Great Shepherd of your life? Take time with God to whisper to him the words of Psalm 23: "The LORD is my shepherd" (v. 1).

Lord Jesus, in these rare moments of quiet with you, allow me to rest in your arms. Tend to me, your sheep.

December 25 has not always been the date of Christmas. In fact, for three centuries after Jesus's sojourn on earth, his birth wasn't much celebrated at all. It was later that the date we observe was arrived at—via an interesting bit of math.

Christian author and patriarch Tertullian, working from the gospel accounts that placed Jesus's crucifixion on 14 Nisan in the Hebrew calendar, calculated the Roman calendar date to be March 25. He then presumed Christ's birth to be on December 25—exactly nine months following. In this way, Jesus was thought to have been conceived and crucified on the same day of the year.

In AD 336, the Christian emperor Constantine, possibly in an effort to compete with other pagan celebrations in winter, established Christmas to be observed on the Tertullian date of December 25.

15

Bethlehem

*The shepherds said to one another, "Let's go to
Bethlehem and see this thing that has happened,
which the Lord has told us about."*

LUKE 2:15

In 1865, Phillips Brooks was the rector at the Church of the Holy Trinity in Philadelphia. For a season of rest and replenishment he took a trip to the Holy Land, and one of the places he visited was the quiet town of Bethlehem.

In a letter to his family he wrote: "[We] took our horses and rode to Bethlehem. It was only about two hours when we came to the town, situated on an eastern ridge of a range of hills, surrounded by its terraced gardens. . . . Before dark, we rode out of town to the field where they say the shepherds saw the star. . . . Somewhere in those fields we rode through the shepherds must have been, and in the same fields the story of Ruth and Boaz must belong."[19]

Two years later, Brooks, reflecting on those moments, wrote the poetry of the Christmas carol "O Little Town of Bethlehem." The last lines of the first verse—"Yet in thy dark streets shineth the everlasting light. The hopes and fears of all the years are met in thee tonight"—must have had a special meaning when Brooks wrote them in 1868, just three years following the hopes and fears of the Civil War.

Bethlehem sits in the shadow of Jerusalem, almost literally, just five miles south of the capital city that dominated Israel's history. Yet this town has its own claim to fame as the site of Rachel's death, Ruth's wedding, and David's upbringing—and of course the birth of Jesus.

The name *Bethlehem* means "house of bread" in Hebrew, though it might instead be an older reference to a Canaanite deity, Lahmi. The area was also known as *Ephrathah*, which means "fruitful" (see Micah 5:2).

Just as Phillips Brooks described, Bethlehem sits along a modest mountain ridge that goes north and south through Israel. An ancient road wends along this ridge, connecting the towns with each other and ultimately with Egypt, Syria, and the rest of the world. In documents from around 1350 BC (the Tell al-Amarna letters), an Egyptian governor described Bethlehem to the pharaoh as an important rest stop for travelers headed to Egypt.

Growing up in Bethlehem, David likely explored the desert canyons to the east and shepherded his flocks in the verdant pasture to the west. His famed fight with Goliath happened in the foothills about fifteen miles west. Later, he hid out in the desert canyons to escape the jealous wrath of King Saul. Once while battling the Philistines, who were encamped in Bethlehem, David's commandos snuck into the town to get David a drink from his favorite well (2 Samuel 23:13–17).

The mountainous terrain around Bethlehem included a number of limestone caves, which were used as shelter for animals. Mary and Joseph likely ended up in one of these. Dwellings were often built into the existing topography, houses incorporating slopes, trees, or caves—and this might have been true of the "inn" as well.

The eastern side of Bethlehem's mountain ridge had desert winds sweeping in from Arabia, drying everything. Dusty canyons descended starkly to the Dead Sea—"a dry and parched land where there is no water" (Psalm 63:1). But Bethlehem settles on the west side of the ridge, where fertile terraces of farmland and grassy foothills slope gently to the coastal plain of the Mediterranean Sea. Wet winds glide in from the sea, get stopped by the mountains, and dump rain on the welcoming soil.

This cove-like feature of the town of Bethlehem makes it all the more special in the context of Jesus's birth. Our awe of this event—God becoming human—is driven home by the specificity of geography. God chose a specific place in all the earth to become incarnated as one of us.

What location in all the earth would that be? This sleepy town of Bethlehem, a fertile cove of a town, sheltered from harsh, dry winds. This same Bethlehem of which Phillips Brooks wrote, "How still we see thee lie! Above thy deep and dreamless sleep the silent stars go by."

Preparing for Christmas

Where is your Bethlehem today? That is, where is your sheltered cove of peace and rest? This Christmas season, can you find a time and place away from the civil-war conflicts of family and friends to make room for Jesus?

Lord Jesus, I welcome you into my quiet place. Sit with me right now. I wish to share with you the hopes and fears of all my years . . .

Experts guess that five hundred to one thousand people lived in Bethlehem at the time of the nativity (though that number might have swelled temporarily if many Davidic descendants were returning for the census). With that population, the number of baby boys killed by Herod's decree might have been ten to twenty-five.

16

Joseph

When Joseph woke up, he did what the angel of the Lord had commanded him and took Mary home as his wife. But he did not consummate their marriage until she gave birth to a son.

MATTHEW 1:24–25

Joseph was the cool stepdad. He plays an active, supportive role throughout the Christmas story. We owe a great deal to his humble acceptance of God's plans.

Where Luke focuses on Mary, the gospel of Matthew gets inside Joseph's head. The man's fiancée was pregnant, though they had never been intimate. We get our first glimpse of Joseph's character in the fact that he didn't fly into a murderous rage. Wanting to protect Mary's reputation, he planned a quiet breakup (Matthew 1:19).

Murderous rage was an option though. In that culture, an engagement held the legal obligations of marriage. Infidelity was adultery, punishable by stoning. Joseph sought a kinder solution.

In a dream, Joseph got the full story from an angel (vv. 20–21). He went ahead with the marriage, while protecting Mary's virginity.

------ ✦ ------

We, of course, cannot know what was going on inside Joseph's head. But one traditional folk carol imagines just that. "Joseph Was an Old Man" dates from the fifteenth century and is often sung to an Appalachian folk tune. It's also known by the title "The Cherry Tree Carol" and was once sung by Peter, Paul, and Mary.

The lyrics are simple, the tune is lilting, and the premise of picking apples and cherries is childlike. But this poetry reflects the conflict that Joseph must have felt:

> Then Mary said to Joseph,
> So meek and so mild,
>
> "Joseph, gather me some cherries,
> For I am with child."
>
> Then Joseph flew in anger,
> In anger flew he.

In the song-story a stanza later, Joseph seems to become aware of this divine thing that is happening and is ashamed of his rage and calls out to God:

> What have I done, Lord?
> Have mercy on me.

The carol assumes some things about Joseph that aren't literally said in the Bible. However, Scripture tells us that in light of the pregnancy, Joseph intended to divorce Mary. It's hard to interpret this in any other way than that he was deeply troubled by her pregnancy, maybe to a point of anger that Mary, so he assumed, had cheated on him. He was upset enough to want to call the whole thing off.

The Scripture further tells us an angel of the Lord had to appear to Joseph, explain things to him, turn him around, and dissuade him from his divorce plan.

So, while we don't know exactly what Joseph was feeling, it seems natural and human that he would feel hurt and confused, troubled and angry. And we can identify. Part of the precious meaning of the Christmas story is found in the authentic humanity of its characters. We might hope that we could be like Joseph in following God's direction in the midst of extraordinary circumstances and impossible emotions.

There's an interesting, deeper story about Joseph that involves lineage and heritage.

Why was Jesus born in Bethlehem? Because Joseph traced his ancestry to King David, and Bethlehem was the "town of David" (Luke 2:4). When the Roman emperor sent people back to their ancestral homes for a census (v. 1), Joseph loaded up the donkey for a trip south.

Both Matthew and Luke include lengthy genealogies for Joseph, but they differ, and scholars aren't sure why. One theory is that Luke is following Mary's lineage but observes the custom of naming only men. So Joseph, by virtue of his marriage to Mary, adopts her family tree. Another theory is that Matthew is following the royal succession of Israel and lines of legal inheritance, which don't always match up with bloodlines. Thus Joseph may have been the physical son of Heli (Luke 3:23) but adopted as the heir of his uncle Jacob (Matthew 1:16).

Did Joseph, then, have a claim to the throne? Was he a member of the nobility? Clearly not. Everything in the nativity story suggests modest circumstances for Joseph and Mary. Remember that they laid their newborn in an animals' feeding trough. They were not royalty, even though they were parents of the King.

What else do we know about Joseph? Not much. After the birth of Jesus in the gospel accounts, except for the dream telling him to take his family to Egypt, Joseph is, in modern terms, only a plus-one.

He is mentioned with Mary as they take the infant to the temple for dedication (Luke 2:22), and twelve years later when they travel to the temple again (v. 48). People occasionally refer to Jesus as Joseph's son (John 1:45), but we don't see this stepdad in action anymore.

Many assume that Joseph was much older than Mary. The Bible does not say this, though Joseph displays a lot of maturity. And it would not be unusual in those times for an older man, perhaps a widower, to negotiate a marriage contract with a family in the community.

The only other reason to think Joseph was older is that he probably died years before Mary did. Since he does not appear in any stories of the adult Jesus—and Mary goes solo in some of those stories—we assume he died sometime between Jesus's thirteenth and thirtieth birthdays.

Joseph lived long enough to teach Jesus a trade: carpentry (Matthew 13:55; Mark 6:3). The Greek word for this kind of tradesman is *tekton*, and the "tek-nology" of that time was not only wood but stone and clay as well. Joseph and Jesus should be seen as builders, as craftsmen, creating homes, tools, and furnishings from all available materials.

There's a poetic parallel in that. Because of his faith and faithfulness, Joseph built a life for Mary and her son Jesus. Because of his faith and faithfulness, Jesus builds a life for us.

Preparing for Christmas

Russell Moore writes, "Joseph was unique in one sense. None of us will ever be called to be father to God. But in another very real sense, Joseph's faith was exactly the same as ours."[20]

We will never encounter the unique circumstance that Joseph did. But we all will be confronted with events we do not expect, that take us by surprise. What will your faith look like in the earthquakes of life? How will you respond to events that might seem to overwhelm you?

Will your faith remain strong, like Joseph's?

Lord God, I ask for this coming year that my faith may be made strong, that I would remain faithful in the face of difficult circumstances, and that I might always keep my eyes on you.

17

Manger

*While they were there, the time came for the baby to
be born, and she gave birth to her firstborn, a son. She
wrapped him in cloths and placed him in a manger,
because there was no guest room available for them.*

LUKE 2:6–7

In the now-classic modern tale *The Best Christmas Pageant Ever*, a
Sunday school director begins planning for the annual Christmas
play. The Herdman children, all six of them, wind up being cast in
the principal parts. This is unfortunate because the Herdman children are all juvenile delinquents, having come to Sunday school
only because they heard there were snacks. The first sentence of
the book tells us, "The Herdmans were absolutely the worst kids
in the history of the world."

Of course, antics and chaos—and humor—ensue. Three
of the Herdman kids, Claude, Ollie, and Leroy, though clueless
about Christmas, are cast as the three wise men.

> "What was the inn?" Claude asked. "What's an inn?"
>   "It's like a motel," somebody told him, "where
> people go to spend the night."

Later, Leroy asks about the manger:

"What was that they laid the baby in?" Leroy said.
"That manger . . . is that like a bed? Why would they
have a bed in the barn?"[21]

We laugh, and yet these are details of the actual Christmas
account that most of us also get wrong. In some ways, we're as
clueless as the Herdmans.

It's amazing how many parts of the Christmas story are not
in the Bible.

There's no innkeeper, for instance. Every Christmas pageant
going back to medieval times has had somebody saying, "Sorry, no
room!" But there's no mention of that person in Scripture.

There are no camels or oxen or donkeys mentioned. Just a
lot of sheep.

And this may surprise you: no stable.

All we know is that Jesus's first crib was a manger. A common
feed bin for animals. That's reported in the story. And because
there's a manger, we assume it was in a stable with an assortment
of animals milling about.

The Greek word for "manger" is *phatne*, used three times in
Luke's nativity account. It also occurs later when Jesus argues with
opponents over Sabbath day regulations: "Doesn't each of you on
the Sabbath untie your ox or donkey from the stall [*phatne*] and
lead it out to give it water?" (Luke 13:15). This connects some dots
in the Christmas story, suggesting that it was common for people
to have at least one "ox or donkey," kept and fed near their homes.
(Maybe we can keep the stable and the friendly beasts after all.)

The main Hebrew word for "manger" (*ebus*) appears in Job 39:9, which suggests that mangers were used for domesticated beasts "at night." During the day, presumably, oxen and donkeys could graze, but they'd be brought inside at night for safekeeping and feeding. As with any domesticated animal, "the donkey [knows] its owner's manger" (Isaiah 1:3).

Mangers were generally basins or troughs chiseled out of stone or formed naturally by the elements. (The limestone that was so prevalent in Israel could be hewn rather easily.) Archaeologists have found some such basins in ancient caves that were used as stables.

We should probably rethink our idea of the "inn" that had no room for the holy family. The word Luke uses is *kataluma*, which elsewhere refers to the guest room of a house. As Jesus prepared for the Last Supper with his disciples, he told them to ask a particular homeowner if his *kataluma* (guest room) was available (Mark 14:14; Luke 22:11). A related word is used when Jesus invites himself to be a guest in the home of Zacchaeus (Luke 19:7).

These situations are similar to the Bethlehem event, and it's clear that these are homes and not hotels (or motels, as the Herdman kids thought). There are other Greek words for "inn." The Good Samaritan takes the robbery victim to a *pandocheion* along the Jerusalem–Jericho road and pays the *pandochei* (Luke 10:34–35). (There's the innkeeper we banished from the Christmas pageant!) Another Greek "inn" word (*xenia*) emphasizes that such an establishment is a place for foreigners (Acts 28:23).

But the Christmas account doesn't use those words. The "inn" referred to in some Bible versions of the Christmas account is a *kataluma*, which more modern versions correctly translate as "guest room," suggesting instead that there was no room in a home owned by relatives or friends of Mary or Joseph.

The fact that the home had a guest room tells us that the hosts were not poor. The style of the time was to build living quarters in two stories around a central courtyard. People would sleep upstairs.

If the household animals weren't kept in a nearby cave, they might be brought into the courtyard at night. The feeding area would often be placed underneath the sleeping quarters so the heat from the animals would keep the family and guests comfortable.

It's possible that Mary and Joseph left the crowded guest room and just went downstairs to the animal-feeding area. Or they were turned away by an overwhelmed host (possibly a relative) who showed them to a nearby cave where the animals were kept safe.

So, as you rewrite your Christmas play, the "inn" was certainly not a motel with a neon sign blinking "No Vacancy." You might more accurately place it in a double-booked bed-and-breakfast, or a family reunion where Aunt Liz just can't fit in another cot.

But, yes, there may have been oxen and donkeys thrown off their feeding schedule and maybe a few horses nuzzling the newborn Savior.

In that, we find the meaning of the manger.

It's echoed through a lot of Christmas carols, but "Away in a Manger" paints the picture as well as any: "The little Lord Jesus asleep on the hay. . . . The cattle are lowing, the baby awakes." Among the dirt and feed and smells of animals, Jesus Christ, the Savior of the world, was born into the humblest of circumstances.

He is one of us.

Preparing for Christmas

Perhaps this is a time for you when you feel the pressure of being perfect. Maybe you're the host for a Christmas party or the chef for Christmas dinner. You worry about the presentation, the decorations, the meal all being right and perfect. You fret about gifts under the tree being enough and looking as if they're wrapped elegantly.

Take a break from all that perfection pressure. Remind yourself that at the most important Christmas ever, Jesus was born in a lowly manger among sheep. The only perfect person in all of history was born to earth in a most imperfect setting. So leave your worries of being perfectly presentable behind. Jesus in the manger is all that matters.

Lord God, thank you for your humble entrance into my world. It reminds me that life doesn't have to be perfect or elegant. Help me in this season to let go of things I obsess about.

Historians believe the first public nativity scene was created by Francis of Assisi in 1223. The idea came to him that some sort of display could effect a public "kindling of devotion" to Jesus Christ. In the Italian town of Greccio, Francis "made ready a manger, and bade hay, together with an ox and an ass, be brought unto the spot,"[22] and speculation has it that he used real people to play Mary, Joseph, and the shepherds. In other words, Francis may have created the first Christmas pageant ever.

18

Impossible

With man this is impossible, but with
God all things are possible.

MATTHEW 19:26

"Do you believe in miracles? Yes!"

As the seconds ticked down on an improbable victory of the US hockey team over the heavily favored Soviets in the 1980 Winter Olympics, announcer Al Michaels uttered that phrase, cementing it in the American consciousness.

But lots of people don't believe in miracles, and that prevents them from taking the Bible seriously. Parting the sea, walking on water, calling fire from heaven—these reports seem too strange to accept. And the virgin birth of Jesus? That's a stumbling block for many.

Yet Luke seems to anticipate such skepticism with his own version of that hockey call: "With God nothing will be impossible" (Luke 1:37 NKJV). If you believe in a God who created the world to begin with, is it crazy to think he rewrites the laws of nature occasionally? Are these strange, out-of-the-ordinary experiences? Yes. That's what *miracle* means. Are they impossible? Maybe according to our natural understanding. But when God is in the picture, anything can happen.

Let's get some context. The angel Gabriel has just announced to Mary that she will bear a child, though she's a virgin. But then he mentions her relative Elizabeth, who "is going to have a child in her old age" (Luke 1:36). Though she thought she was unable to conceive, she is already in her sixth month of pregnancy. See, Mary? Nothing is impossible with God.

This wasn't the first time God had granted a seemingly impossible birth to an elderly couple. In Genesis, we see three "men" (probably angels) visiting the aged Abraham and Sarah and announcing that they will have a child. In disbelief, Sarah laughs—which is why they name the child *Isaac* (which means "laughter"). In response to her laugh, an angel asks, "Is anything too hard for the LORD?" (18:14).

Here's a connection that might be new to you.

Luke (and possibly Mary) would have been familiar with the Greek version of the Old Testament (the Septuagint). There, the angel says to Abraham, "Shall any thing [*rema*] be impossible [*adunatesei*] with God [*para to theo*]?"

Now, in the New Testament, the angel tells Mary, "No thing [*rema*] is impossible [*adunatesei*] with God [*para to theo*]" (see Luke 1:37). Gabriel seems to be acting from the same script.

The New Testament takes us on what we might call a journey of possibility—and impossibility—beginning with the miraculous birth of Jesus. As an adult, Jesus worked miracles that seemed impossible—multiplying meals, calming a storm—yet some of his greatest miracles involved the transformation of people's hearts. After saying how difficult it was for rich people to get to heaven, Jesus added, "With man this is impossible, but with God all things are possible" (Matthew 19:26; see also Mark 10:27; Luke 18:27).

We see Jesus's journey of possibility continue as he prayed in

Gethsemane before his death, "My Father, if it is not possible for this cup [suffering] to be taken away unless I drink it, may your will be done" (Matthew 26:42; see also v. 39). This reflects Jesus's humanity ("Could it be possible I will not suffer?") as well as his divinity ("No, it is not possible, so your will be done").

He went willingly to the cross, "but God raised him from the dead, freeing him from the agony of death, because it was impossible for death to keep its hold on him" (Acts 2:24). So preached Peter on the day of Pentecost. It's fascinating that this seemingly impossible event—resurrection from the dead—was actually inevitable. It couldn't *not* happen, because Jesus was Lord even over death.

The sacrifice of Jesus changed everything, challenging the previous ways of worship. The book of Hebrews strongly states, "It is impossible for the blood of bulls and goats to take away sins" (10:4). People would connect with God in a new way, through faith in Jesus. "And without faith it is impossible to please God, because anyone who comes to him must believe that he exists and that he rewards those who earnestly seek him" (Hebrews 11:6).

Faith in Jesus not only brings us salvation but also empowers our lives in amazing ways. As Jesus said, "If you have faith as small as a mustard seed, you can say to this mountain, 'Move from here to there,' and it will move. Nothing will be impossible for you" (Matthew 17:20). Elsewhere he remarked, "Everything is possible for one who believes" (Mark 9:23).

That might sound like a magic wand we use to get whatever we want, but it's more than that. We trust in God's power to do God's work in the world. Like Jesus in the garden, we submit to what the Father wants.

Do you believe in miracles? Yes! We trust in the God who specializes in doing the impossible.

Placide Cappeau was a wine merchant in France in 1847. He'd lost his right hand in a shooting accident as a boy. He was also something of a poet. Although Cappeau was nonreligious and a self-proclaimed atheist, he was commissioned by the local priest to write a poem commemorating the refurbishing of the church pipe organ. The resulting work carried the title "Minuit, Chrétiens" ("Midnight, Christians").

Cappeau approached a composer friend of his, Adolphe Adam, to put the poem to music. Adam was known for his operas and ballets. He happened to be a Jew and certainly was not a believer in Jesus Christ. But he composed a tune for Cappeau's poem.[23]

Later, in America, John Sullivan Dwight, a music critic and political socialist,[24] discovered Cappeau's song, translated it into English, gave it a new title, and launched it into popularity.

That is how a one-handed atheist poet, a Jewish opera composer, and an American socialist created one of the most beloved of all Christmas carols—"O Holy Night."

Who says God can't do the impossible?

Preparing for Christmas

What is the impossible thing in your life that God has made happen? What is the miracle you need today? Consider the "impossibility" of God becoming human flesh in the birth of Jesus. What circumstance in your life, then, is too big for God?

Lord God, thank you for reminding me of the greatest miracle of all. Help me hold close to my heart the possibility you provide me in my everyday life.

19

Caesar

*In those days Caesar Augustus issued a decree that a
census should be taken of the entire Roman world.*

LUKE 2:1

We often focus on the spiritual meaning of Christmas, and that's
good. But let's not forget the political reality: the Son of God was
born into a world dominated by a powerful empire, ruled by a
Caesar who was often hailed as a god himself.

The conflict between Christ and Caesar (and worldly power
in general) is a common theme in Scripture. Paul reminds us,
"Though we live in the world, we do not wage war as the world
does. The weapons we fight with are not the weapons of the
world" (2 Corinthians 10:3–4).

Indeed, the decisive blow against all the Caesars of the world
came on a quiet night in Bethlehem.

Caesar enters the Christmas story in the first line of Luke 2:
"In those days Caesar Augustus issued a decree that a census should
be taken of the entire Roman world." He was the most powerful
man in the empire—at least until the baby was laid in the manger.

Yet Caesar was not just a man but the figurehead of an empire
that embodied all the power, glory, and shame of humanity. The
Caesar story starts a generation before that night in Bethlehem.

Already a respected general and consul in the Roman Republic, Julius Caesar moved to take more decisive powers in the years 49 to 45 BC. The name Caesar was just his name, not yet a title.

After Julius was assassinated in 44 BC, a power struggle raged for years. But he had designated a grandnephew, Octavian, as his heir. Claiming his inherited right to the Caesar name, Octavian fought off his foes (especially Mark Antony and Cleopatra) and was declared emperor in 27 BC, taking the name *Augustus* ("venerable"). Thereafter, he was generally known as Augustus Caesar.

This was the Caesar in power when Jesus was born.

The Augustan age is hailed by historians as a time of peace and power for Rome (which was the beginning of what is known as the Pax Romana). The imperial army was strong enough to intimidate would-be rebels. On the Mediterranean Sea, the navy kept piracy in check. Roads were built throughout the empire to ensure that troops could quickly get to any trouble spot. In many corners of the realm, local rulers were put in charge, as long as they paid taxes and cooperated with Rome. (This was the case with King Herod of Judea, who was an old pal of Octavian's.)

When Augustus Caesar died, he passed the Caesar name—and its power—to his stepson, who became Tiberius Caesar. From this point forward, the name became a title for the emperor of Rome. In fact, over the centuries it entered the vocabulary of several languages as a term for any absolute ruler. Russia had *czars*. Germany had *kaisers*. Both these words derive from *Caesar*. The Greek spelling is *Kaisar*.

When his opponents tried to trip up Jesus with a trick question about taxes, he asked for a coin. It had Caesar's head engraved on it. The trick in the question had to do with the fact that Caesar was also self-described as divine.

"Render to Caesar the things that are Caesar's," Jesus famously said, "and to God the things that are God's" (Mark 12:17 KJV). This seems like Jesus is deferring to Caesar. But many have interpreted his response to mean, "Give Tiberius your coins; give God your hearts." In a clever way, our Lord is saying, "Let Caesar have his place, but God is above all."

The quiet birth of Jesus in Bethlehem was a tsunami that would change the world—both in spite of and because of the Caesars.

The New Testament covers a period roughly equivalent to five Caesars who ruled over the developing Roman Empire. Jesus was born under Augustus Caesar and died (and rose again) under Tiberius. Caligula had a very short reign, and Claudius Caesar was in power when Paul began his missionary journeys. Nero was the Caesar that the apostle Paul appealed to in Acts 25 and was the hand behind the brutal executions of Peter and Paul.

We might wonder why God chose this time and place for Jesus's birth. Why then? Why under the rule of the Caesars in the heart of the Roman Empire?

We go back to the Pax Romana, a period of about two hundred years that began under the first emperor, Augustus. The leaders of Rome, though brutal as heads of state, presided over an expanding empire and a stable government.

This situation of relative peace and great mobility made it easy for the Christian movement to spread through the empire.

The Caesars unwittingly paved the way (literally, by building roads) for the birth of Christianity.

The Caesars may have laughed at Jesus and his followers, but it seems God had the last laugh.

Preparing for Christmas

At Christmas, fortunately, we don't sing carols that speak of Augustus Caesar. Well, there *is* one age-old carol titled "When Caesar Augustus Had Rais'd a Taxation" (yes, for real), but we're guessing that will never make it onto *Billboard*'s top ten yuletide tunes.

Instead, we might find a Caesar connection in one of the choruses in George Handel's *Messiah*. "For unto Us a Child Is Born" is taken from Isaiah 9:6: "For unto us a child is born, unto us a son is given: and the government shall be upon his shoulder: and his name shall be called Wonderful, Counsellor, The mighty God, The everlasting Father, The Prince of Peace" (KJV).

Take a moment to ponder this: the Jesus child, born under a Caesar, would outlast them all and take on the government of the whole world. "Of the increase of his government and peace there shall be no end" (v. 7 KJV).

> *God of all, God of my life, I kneel before you in awe of your greatness. Thank you for Jesus, the Prince of Peace.*

The Roman historian Pliny the Elder suggested that Julius Caesar had an ancestor who was cut out of the womb at his birth—a Caesarean section, related to the Latin word for "cutting." If he's right, the royal name came from the procedure and not vice versa.

It's no surprise to read that "Caesar Augustus issued a decree" related to taxation (Luke 2:1). The problem is that we have no other historical record of this decree. It might be better to see it as a policy of orderly census-taking and taxing that Augustus demanded of those ruling provinces throughout the "Roman world." That would fit the organized style of this emperor. The ancient historian Tacitus reported that, at his death in AD 14, Augustus left many documents with statistics on population and taxation. It seems he was a data hound.

20
Good News

But the angel said to them, "Do not be afraid. I bring
you good news that will cause great joy for all the people.
Today in the town of David a Savior has been born to
you; he is the Messiah, the Lord."

LUKE 2:10–11

"I've got good news and bad news." That's the setup for one of the oldest gags on the comedy circuit.

But an angel takes the stage in the Bethlehem sky and says to some flabbergasted shepherds, "I've got good news."

No bad news. No catch, no punch line. Just joyous good news for everyone on earth. It's happening this very night. The promised Messiah is here.

And, by the way, he's here to save us.

"I bring good news" is contained in just one word in Greek, *euangelizomai*. Don't try to pronounce it, but let's dissect it. The word *angel* in the middle means "report." That's what angels are—messengers, news bringers, reporting on what God is thinking and doing.

The prefix *eu* means "good." We see it in words like *eulogy* (good words said at someone's funeral), *euphoria* (a good feeling),

97

and *euphemism* (good phrasing instead of the bad phrase you want to say). Since Greek really doesn't have an equivalent for the letter *v*, the letter *u* (the Greek upsilon) often moves into English as a *v*. So *euangelizomai* becomes "evangelize."

You might say this angel was the first evangelist.

Except Isaiah was all over this good news several centuries earlier. Beginning in chapter 40, this prophet crowed about the message of redemption God was speaking to his captive people:

> You who bring good news to Zion,
>   go up on a high mountain.
> You who bring good news to Jerusalem,
>   lift up your voice with a shout,
> lift it up, do not be afraid;
>   say to the towns of Judah,
>   "Here is your God!"
> See, the Sovereign LORD comes with power.
>   (vv. 9–10)

Here we see a fascinating aspect of Hebrew thinking. God talks about what he's doing *as he does it*. He says, "Let there be light," and there's light (Genesis 1:3). He blesses Abraham verbally and creates an eternal relationship (Genesis 12:1–3). He says (through Moses), "Let my people go," and forces the pharaoh to do so (Exodus 5:1). The announcement of redemption *is a part of* that redemption.

So it's no surprise that the birth of Jesus is heralded by God's messenger. "Let there be salvation!" And there is a Savior.

Isaiah wrote about a special servant of God appointed to "proclaim good news to the poor" (61:1). Jesus quoted this verse at the beginning of his ministry (Luke 4:18) and used the phrase often as he went from town to town (see 4:43; 7:22).

What was this "good news to the poor"? At minimum, it was the assurance that God had not forgotten his people. It's tough to be poor, but God had a better life in store for them. In Jesus's teaching, the good news was often connected with the kingdom of God, which was full of surprising turnabouts. In God's coming kingdom, the poor and humble would be favored over the rich and arrogant. This was indeed good news for poor folks who had been treated unfairly.

But there's much, much more. Jesus was not just the bringer of good news; he *was* the Good News. This is what the angel was saying to the slack-jawed shepherds. Jesus was not just a reminder of God's love; he was the demonstration of it. As the events of Jesus's ministry unfolded—his death and resurrection—the good news took on a new meaning.

The early Christians "never stopped teaching and proclaiming the good news that Jesus is the Messiah" (Acts 5:42). The word for "good news" is used five times in Acts 8 as the Christian movement bursts out of Judea, and many times more in the rest of Acts and the Epistles. "For I am not ashamed of the gospel [*euangelion*]," Paul writes, "because it is the power of God that brings salvation to everyone who believes: first to the Jew, then to the Gentile. For in the gospel the righteousness of God is revealed" (Romans 1:16–17).

Far more than "Don't worry, be happy," the good news is "Look at the amazing thing God has done in Jesus Christ!"

And so it's appropriate that the opening words of the book of Mark are "The beginning of the good news [*euangelion*] about Jesus the Messiah" (1:1). Everything Jesus said and did was wrapped up in this amazing news of God's redemption.

That's why we call the first four books of the New Testament *the Gospels*. They tell the story of the salvation-event of Jesus.

And in the telling, the salvation spreads.

Noël is French for "Christmas." It seems to have morphed from the Latin *natalis* ("birth") and through an early French elision *na'el*. But the term might also be influenced by another French word, *nouvelle*, which means "new" or "news."

Supporting this thought is the weird word order of the opening line of a favorite Christmas carol: "The first Noel the angel did say was to certain poor shepherds in fields as they lay." (It's almost Yoda-like: "Much to learn you still have.") If that lyric simply means "Christmas," it makes little sense. But if it means "good news," then it comes together.

Here's a suggestion: try singing the chorus of "The First Noel" by substituting "Good news!" in place of the word "Noel!"

Preparing for Christmas

Perhaps there's a lesson for us in all that word study. Are we just celebrating a "Noel Christmas" with all its traditions and trappings and holiday busyness? Or are we proclaiming the "Noel good news" that lies at the heart of what Christmas truly means?

What can you do in this Christmas season to ground yourself in the deeper biblical meaning of the good news that brings great joy?

Lord God, help me step away from the craziness of Christmas to focus on the "good news" meaning of Noel. Bring me back to the moment when the news of who Jesus is first broke into my life.

The word *noel* has another related meaning—"a Christmas song or carol." And so it would be proper to say, "The choir sang noels at the Christmas Eve service."

21
Ponder

They will proclaim the works of God and
ponder what he has done.

PSALM 64:9

If you'll allow us a personal remembrance, a few Christmases ago, the two of us gathered with our sister and our ninety-year-old father. Dad only had energy for a couple of hours, but we enjoyed a nice dinner and then talked. We all had the feeling that we might not have many more holidays together, and so we three offspring peppered him with questions about his life. What was it like growing up in the Great Depression? When did he first get involved in church leadership? Where did his love of music come from?

Some of these things we already knew, but we were gathering this information one last time. In a few months, the facility where Dad lived shut down due to COVID, and within the next year he had succumbed to the pandemic. But we treasured these last conversations with him, tossed around memories, and *pondered* these things in our hearts. We still do, as we remember our amazing father with love and joy.

The word *ponder*, for us and in Scripture, carries a sense of cherishing memories, a kind of meditative wonder. As we ponder a life, we hold close to our hearts things we don't ever want to forget.

Our experience was toward the end of our dad's remarkable life and steadfast faith. For Mary the mother of Jesus, pondering took place at the end of a hectic night. Traveling, finding a place, bearing the child, being visited by shepherds. That was a lot to take in, and she gathered it all: "But Mary treasured up all these things and pondered them in her heart" (Luke 2:19).

The word for "treasured" (*suntereo*) has the sense of protecting, guarding, perhaps hoarding a treasure. She didn't want to lose these memories. In that verse, there's some ambiguity with the word for "things" (*rema*). Sometimes it means "words," sometimes "things." The shepherds had just shared the angelic announcement. A Savior. Good news for all people. So Mary might have gathered these heavenly words as validation of her own encounter with an angel some nine months earlier. Or she might have been treasuring the whole experience in her mental scrapbook.

In any case, Mary "pondered" them. This word (*sumballo*) literally means "throw together" or maybe "toss around." We get a word picture of these memories bouncing around her mind and soul as she tries to make sense of what has happened to her.

Mary's pondering came at the beginning of her son's life. We can only wonder how these thoughts and memories stirred within her soul as he grew. We get glimpses . . .

As she takes her baby to be dedicated at the temple, a prophet has visions of grandeur for the infant but mentions that a sword will pierce her soul. More to ponder here . . .

The twelve-year-old Jesus stows away in the temple, explaining that he has his Father's work to attend to. Clearly not carpentry. *So this is what it's like to mother a Messiah*, Mary ponders . . .

Mary urges the grown-up Jesus to save a wedding party that

has disastrously run out of wine. Does a mother have the right to prod her son into action? Normally yes, but shouldn't a Savior already know what to do? Mary makes a subtle request and Jesus resists . . . and then responds. His miracle ministry begins, and Mary has even more to ponder . . .

Watching her son's gruesome death, she might have wondered, *Is this the sword that will pierce my soul? It sure feels that way . . .*

We don't know whether she was one of the Marys who came to the tomb on Resurrection Sunday, but she was meeting with the Jesus followers before the Pentecost event (Acts 1:14). What was going through her mind during these stunning occurrences? Perhaps she flashed back to that day in Nazareth when an angel interrupted her ordinary life . . .

We don't know what Mary was pondering, of course, but there's intrigue that makes us wonder. What did she know and when? Was this a gradual revealing of the ultimate plot of Scripture, or did her virgin birth immediately make her aware of the divine plan?

A contemporary Christmas carol muses on what Mary may have known, what she was aware of throughout her son's life. "Mary, Did You Know?" recounts some of the events of Jesus's ministry, asking the question of what she knew and when.[25]

Did Mary know who her son was when he calmed the storm and when he gave sight to a blind man?

Did she know that the child she bore would be the Christ who would someday deliver *her*? Did she know that this child born among lambs was indeed the Lamb of God?

The carol is utterly beautiful and brings us into the humanity of Mary and what she pondered.

Preparing for Christmas

Make this season a time to ponder what God has done in your life. Long ago, what did you know of him? When did you know he was God? When did he become the God of your life? Toss around these memories, cherish them, hold them close to your heart. Speak them aloud to the Lord of your life.

*Lord God, thank you for the many things
you've done in my life . . .*

The Greek word for "ponder" in Luke 2:19 is translated in several different ways, depending on the context. Jesus uses this word for how kings "make" war (Luke 14:31 NKJV). When Paul brought his strange new ideas to Athens, the local Stoic philosophers began to "debate" with him (Acts 17:18). That's the same word—*sumballo*. It can also mean a meeting or discussion. This range of meanings drives us back to the Greek root. *Sumballo* means "throw together," whether that's armies thrown together in battle or a council batting around ideas, conferring (or debating) about what to do next. Or it might be a woman conferring with herself, within her own soul, sifting through her feelings to see what they all mean.

22
Magnificat

My soul glorifies the Lord and my spirit
rejoices in God my Savior.

LUKE 1:46-47

The Magnificat refers to Mary's spoken response to the news that she is bearing the Christ child. This passage in Luke 1:46–55 is sometimes called "Mary's Song" or "The Prayer of Mary." Put to music in the church from earliest times, the Magnificat is considered a *canticle*—Scripture sung in worship.

These words of Mary are among the most personal, deeply emotional expressions of faith in the Bible. Perhaps that's why we identify with them so.

The circumstance for this utterance by Mary is a visit with her cousin Elizabeth, who is also miraculously pregnant. The two women share their experiences, both of them aware of the divine nature of their pregnancies. Elizabeth, filled with the Holy Spirit, proclaims to Mary, "Blessed are you among women . . ." (Luke 1:42).

Mary then launches into song. This seems to have come up naturally in that conversation, though Mary (or Luke) might have taken thoughts from that chat and composed the song later. In any case, those lyrics have become known as the Magnificat.

The word is not Greek or Hebrew, like so many of the other words we have examined. It's Latin, *magnificat* being the first word of this song in the Vulgate translation of the Bible used in the Roman church for centuries. (That version, by the way, was primarily created by Jerome around AD 400, doing much of his work in Bethlehem.)

"Magnificat anima mea Dominum," the song begins in Latin.

In the original Greek, it's "Megalunei he psuche mou ton Kurion."

The King James Version brings it into English as "My soul doth magnify the Lord."

The word *magnify* yields the term *Magnificat*.

While the idea of magnifying someone seems strange to modern ears (unless you're working with their picture in Photoshop), it's a very accurate translation of the Greek (and Latin) phrasing.

The root meaning of the Greek word *megaluno* is to make something bigger, to extend a schedule or expand a job description. Jesus chided the Pharisees for enlarging (*megaluno*) the hem of their robes to set themselves apart from less religious folks (Matthew 23:5). Paul told the Corinthians how he planned to expand (*megaluno*) his ministry and "preach the gospel in the regions beyond you" (2 Corinthians 10:16).

Contemplating his own death, Paul prayed that "Christ will be exalted [*megaluno*] in my body, whether by life or by death" (Philippians 1:20). Here we see the term used in the way Mary used it: to praise or honor someone, in essence to make their reputation greater (see Acts 5:13; 10:46; 19:17).

The Magnificat is a great piece of work. As a hymn of praise, it's beautiful, but it's far more than that. It's a revolutionary manifesto. Mary is grateful that God has thought of her in her meager circumstances, but she also seems very aware that her child will turn the world upside down:

> He has scattered those who are proud in their
> inmost thoughts.
> He has brought down rulers from their thrones
> but has lifted up the humble.
> He has filled the hungry with good things
> but has sent the rich away empty. (Luke 1:51–53)

The tone is very similar to a song by another woman who was surprised to be with child—Samuel's mother, Hannah. She had been childless a long time, a matter of great shame in her culture. She prayed and prayed and promised to give her child back to the Lord if he would grant her one. He did. "My heart rejoices in the Lord," Hannah's song began (1 Samuel 2:1).

But Hannah also sang about social upheaval:

> The bows of the warriors are broken,
> but those who stumbled are armed with strength.
> Those who were full hire themselves out for food,
> but those who were hungry are hungry no more. . . .
>
> The Lord sends poverty and wealth;
> he humbles and he exalts.
> He raises the poor from the dust
> and lifts the needy from the ash heap. (vv. 4–5, 7–8)

Both Mary and Hannah lived in an Israel that was dominated by foreigners—Philistines for Hannah, Romans for Mary. Both saw their miracle babies as promises from God, assurances that he had not forgotten his people, that he would punish the proud oppressors and rescue the needy ones who trusted him.

As it turned out, Hannah's child grew up to be the prophet who anointed a young David as king of Israel. Mary's child—the son of David—accomplished a redemption that even Mary couldn't have foreseen.

And our lives are changed forever.

Luke indulges in a bit of wordplay a few verses after Mary's song. Elizabeth had her miracle baby, John the Baptist. Neighbors and relatives celebrated with her, because "the Lord had shown her *great mercy*" (Luke 1:58, emphasis added). Actually, Luke is using our old friend *megaluno*. It suggests that in Elizabeth's experience, God was magnifying his mercy to her. Perhaps Luke is reminding us that as we magnify the name of the Lord, he magnifies his blessings to us.

Preparing for Christmas

The words of the Magnificat have been put to music by countless composers in a multitude of musical styles, from Gregorian chant to hard rock. Most versions are hard to sing as a Christmas song. But many are beautiful to listen to.

For a devotional time, you might look up one version of the Magnificat by Keith and Kristyn Getty, which uses the haunting Irish tune of the "Wexford Carol" as a musical frame.[26] As you listen to this (or another version of the Magnificat) ponder your own God-wonders.

Take quiet time to magnify him. And consider how he has magnified you. What has he done in your life? What has he rescued you from? What has he provided you? Speak your own magnificat to him.

My soul magnifies you, Lord. You have filled me with good things. Expand my life with your presence.

23
Marvel

Now when they had seen Him, they made widely
known the saying which was told them concerning
this Child. And all those who heard it marveled at
those things which were told them by the shepherds.

LUKE 2:17-18 NKJV

Have you entered the Marvel Universe? Starting as a comic book company, Marvel has been churning out blockbuster films in recent years, featuring different superheroes who operate in the same fictional world. Iron Man, Captain America, Black Widow, Shang-Chi, Thor, and others dazzle moviegoers with their abilities (and the filmmakers' special effects). If, while reading the book of Judges, you've wondered why they were called *judges*, note that the word might be better translated "avengers." They fought for justice against the nation's enemies . . . But that's another word study for another book.

In real life, we might marvel at an athletic performance (Steph Curry hits another trey from mid-court!), or a stirring speech ("I Have a Dream"), or soaring music (Beethoven's Ninth Symphony floors us every time). In such experiences, we are transported out of the everyday.

How is this possible? It isn't normal! We go through life expecting the ordinary. And so we marvel when *extraordinary* happens.

Angels appearing to shepherds—now that's extraordinary. A Savior coming as a baby, gurgling in a manger—not a normal occurrence. So when the shepherds told their friends and families, and probably anyone else who would listen, "all those who heard it marveled at those things which were told them by the shepherds" (Luke 2:18 NKJV). Other translations say they "wondered" or "were amazed."

The Greek word used there is *thaumazo*, which appears in various forms about fifty times in the New Testament and another hundred times in the Greek translation of the Old Testament.

It seems the Bible is full of amazing things.

Throughout Scripture, amazement is a common response to the acts of God. Before the crossing of the Jordan River and the battle of Jericho, Joshua announces, "Consecrate yourselves, for tomorrow the Lord will do amazing things among you" (Joshua 3:5).

Through the prophet Habakkuk, the Lord invites observers to be "utterly amazed" at what he does. "For I am going to do something in your days that you would not believe, even if you were told" (1:5).

A psalmist proclaims, "The stone the builders rejected has become the cornerstone; the Lord has done this, and it is marvelous in our eyes" (Psalm 118:22–23). In the New Testament, this image is often applied to Jesus (see Matthew 21:42).

In the Gospels, we see Jesus astonishing people at every turn. When Jesus spoke in his hometown synagogue, "all spoke well of him and were amazed at the gracious words that came from his lips. 'Isn't this Joseph's son?' they asked" (Luke 4:22). Later, when he began to teach in the temple courts, people "were amazed and asked, 'How did this man get such learning without having been taught?'" (John 7:15).

But it wasn't just his teaching that made people marvel. "The people were amazed when they saw the mute speaking, the crippled made well, the lame walking and the blind seeing. And they praised the God of Israel" (Matthew 15:31).

You might think that Jesus's closest followers would get used to him, but he regularly surprised them too. After he calmed a dangerous storm at sea, "in fear and amazement they asked one another, 'Who is this? He commands even the winds and the water, and they obey him'" (Luke 8:25).

Jesus also amazed people in quieter ways. His disciples expressed surprise that he chatted with a Samaritan woman (John 4:27). And at his trial, "Jesus made no reply, not even to a single charge—to the great amazement of the governor [Pilate]" (Matthew 27:14).

Marveling is shown as an appropriate response to Jesus and what God has done through him. A vision in the Bible's final book shows victorious believers offering glory to God: "Great and marvelous are your deeds, Lord God Almighty" (Revelation 15:3).

In one epistle, Paul looks forward to "the day [Jesus] comes to be glorified in his holy people and to be marveled at among all those who have believed. This includes you, because you believed our testimony to you" (2 Thessalonians 1:10).

We return to the wonder of Christ's birth, knowing this is the focal point of all the marvel in the Bible, in history, and in our lives today. If there was an "Oh my!" moment when time seemed to stand still, this was it. If there was a warp in history when God stepped through, this was it. If there was a time when heaven's joy was felt by those manger-side and us cross-side, this was it.

Our amazement lies not just in the intricate arrangements of space and time and prophecy that aligned for the birth of Jesus Christ, or even in the very idea of the incarnation, God becoming human like us—though those are nothing less than astonishing. Our amazement lies in the fact that all of this comes from *God's love*. He loved us so much that he sent his only Son.

This, then, is the marvel we sing about at Christmas in the carol "Joy to the World," especially the final stanza:

> He rules the world with truth and grace
> And makes the nations prove
> The glories of His righteousness
> And wonders of His love,
> And wonders of His love,
> And wonders, wonders of His love.

Preparing for Christmas

In passage after passage, the Bible invites you to *thaumazo*. God wants you to marvel. To be astonished. To let him surprise you with his love.

Let this be for you the meaning of the manger. Let this be for you the true marvel of Christmas.

> *Lord God, here are some of the ways you've amazed me in my life . . . I recall the words of Peter: "But you are a chosen people, . . . God's special possession." Thank you, Lord, for your love. May I "declare the praises" of you who called me "out of darkness into [your] wonderful light" (1 Peter 2:9).*

24

Word

In the beginning was the Word, and the Word was with God, and the Word was God.

JOHN 1:1

The word for "word" is more than a word.

You might be familiar with the Greek word *logos*, which is generally translated as "word," but it has a rich history, which enlarges its meaning considerably.

After the angel announced to Mary that she would bear the Christ child, she said, "May your word to me be fulfilled" (Luke 1:38). Later, the shepherds "spread the word concerning what had been told them about this child" (2:17). In both cases, the Greek text uses *rema*, a rather common term for something that has been said. But when the angel first appeared to Mary and blessed her, she "was greatly troubled at his words [*logos*] and wondered what kind of greeting this might be" (1:29).

While *rema* and *logos* are synonyms, we get the sense that *logos* is bigger—not just nouns and verbs but a message, a presentation, an idea. Who would blame this peasant girl for being shocked that an angel would barge into her kitchen and call her "highly favored" (v. 28)? It wasn't just the words that troubled her but the whole message-delivering event.

Logos has two origin stories. We might call one Greek and the other Hebrew.

In Greek, it's the noun form of the verb *lego*. If you think of building blocks, you're not far off. This word goes back to the beginnings of language. The original meaning of *lego* was "to count," which suggests it was used in early bartering. Later it took on other meanings: naming, describing, or explaining.

The noun form, *logos*, was applied then to anything that was counted, named, described, or explained—as if nothing really existed until it was talked about. *Logos* could mean "thing" as well as "word."

Then came the fourth century BC, when Plato and other philosophers blew the roof off reality. In simple terms, they taught that anything we see is a physical image of a heavenly idea of that thing. Later philosophers attached the term *logos* to those heavenly ideas. So the *logos* wasn't just a thing or the word used for that thing. Some began to use *logos* for the *heavenly prototype* for that thing, and the eternal principle that governed the existence of all things.

Apologies to any expert philosophers reading this. We know it's an oversimplification of Platonic thought, but it does provide a bit of context for this amazing Greek word.

Let's now rewind to the Hebrew story of creation found in Genesis 1. One of the first things we learn about the Creator is that he *speaks*—and when he speaks, things leap into existence. Light, oceans, stars, birds, people. God's word has creative power.

As in Greek, Hebrew has several words for "speaking" and "saying." *Dabar* corresponds most closely to *logos*. It means "thing" as well as "word," and it's also used for the "Word of God." So when the Word of the Lord came to Joel (for instance, as with many other prophets), the word for "Word" is *dabar* (see Joel 1:1). More than a dictionary entry, it's God's utterance, his message, his guidance, his way of moving his people forward. "Your word [*dabar*] is a lamp for my feet, a light on my path," the psalmist says (119:105).

And so when we consider "the Word" in Scripture, both the Hebrew *dabar* and the Greek *logos* inform its meaning.

There's a Christmas story we often overlook—not Luke's shepherds or Matthew's magi but John and his marvelous mash-up of Hebrew and Greek philosophy. As he begins his gospel, his Jesus-story, he goes back long before Bethlehem.

"In the beginning was the Word, and the Word was with God, and the Word was God" (John 1:1).

Greek thinkers would nod in agreement. This was what Plato was getting at, an eternal principle that governed all existence, the reason for everything, the heavenly ideal of which everything on earth is just a bad copy.

Hebrew scholars would be nodding too, but for a different reason. John's language mirrors that of Genesis 1. "In the beginning" God spoke the world into being (v. 1). His word was the creative force that made everything. They'd be tracking with John through the next few verses. "In him was life, and that life was the light of all mankind" (John 1:4). Yes, God created light and separated it from darkness. He created life with his powerful Word.

Finally, John gets to his version of the star and the stable: "The Word became flesh and made his dwelling among us" (1:14).

"Whoa!" say the philosophers and rabbis. "Didn't see that coming!" Everything they thought about the divine Word that formed the universe was wrapped up in that well-swaddled baby.

That cooing, puking, pooping eight pounds of flesh was the reason for everything.

When John writes "The Word became flesh," he is leading us to another word about the Word—*incarnation*. This is *really* the core meaning of Christmas. The season is not really about a tree or a turkey or tidings. It's not about family getting together. It's not even about Bethlehem and the manger and wise men. None of it bears any real meaning apart from this one thing—the incarnated Word.

R. C. Sproul said, "What we celebrate at Christmas is not so much the birth of a baby. . . . But what's so significant about the birth of that particular baby is that in this birth we have the incarnation of God himself."[27]

God taking on the flesh of a human being, walking and talking among us, enduring the pangs of hunger and thirst and fatigue and pain—this incarnation is what Christmas is meant to be about.

One nineteenth-century Christmas carol addresses this concept in poetry and music: "The Incarnation" by H. R. Bramley.

> The Word in the bliss of the Godhead remains,
> Yet in flesh comes to suffer the keenest of pains;
> He is that He was, and for ever shall be,
> But becomes that He was not, for you and for me.[28]

This poetry captures the mystery of the Word becoming incarnated in human flesh, God being both present in heaven and present among us. It echoes the exquisite complexity of the incarnation—how Jesus Christ, eternal, became "that He was not," entering time and space "for you and for me."

Preparing for Christmas

Take some time alone, apart, to ponder what the Word means to you. How does the Word of the Lord speak to you? What does it mean to you that the Word (Jesus) is both a heavenly presence and an earthly presence near to you? How do you understand Christmas in the light of the Word being made incarnate?

Lord God, you are the Word spoken, become flesh in Jesus Christ. I want to experience all the meanings wrapped up in the Word incarnated in the baby Jesus. Help me experience your special presence during this season of Christmas.

25
Glory

And suddenly there was with the angel a multitude of the heavenly host praising God and saying: "Glory to God in the highest, and on earth peace, goodwill toward men!"

LUKE 2:13-14 NKJV

The shepherds were minding their own business—literally tending to their sheep-keeping business—when all heaven broke loose. "An angel of the Lord appeared to them, and the glory of the Lord shone around them, and they were terrified" (Luke 2:9).

What exactly was this "glory" that dazzled them? The Greek word, *doxa*, often means "reputation" or "fame," as well as the praise that someone of great fame might receive. (A quarterback might get all the glory for a team's victory.) It can also refer to someone's appearance. (A bride might be decked out in all her glory.)

"The heavens declare the glory of God," the psalmist sings (Psalm 19:1), summing up all these meanings. The celestial expanse offers praise for the greatness of God, but there's also something very visual about it. And that's what we see in the Christmas story. The Lord's glory "shone around" the shepherds. It must have been a dazzling display of light.

Probably the closest thing we have today to this spectacle of glory is a fireworks display.

In America, on the Fourth of July, families gather in parks and fields and parking lots to watch the dazzle of fireworks in the night sky. This celebrates Independence Day, but there are other occasions too—Memorial Day, commemorating veterans who served in wars, and the Olympics, honoring athletes who have achieved greatness. There's also the fireworks display at Disney World against the backdrop of the Magic Kingdom, which celebrates . . . well, we're not sure what.

We thrill to those nighttime displays, respect the significance they have, and stand in awe of the pyrotechnics. And yet all of it is rather manufactured, isn't it? Fireworks are just explosives in color and 3D, sold in large warehouses at the edge of town.

A fireworks display is "glory" bought.

Imagine instead a night sky that lights up of its own (God's) accord, is filled with angels singing, and miraculously shines round us all, as it did round those shepherds in the field. This is not glory bought nor glory we are desperately trying to create but the glory of God himself. This is heaven breaking loose, unable to contain its joy!

The main Hebrew word for "glory" is *kabod*, used 120 times in the Old Testament. The Hebrew language is rooted in the body and the senses (whereas Greek is more idea based), so many Old Testament words connect with experiences or objects. *Kabod* literally means "weight." To be glorious is to be heavy. This probably came from a time when people counted out money by weight or bartered with livestock according to how big the animals were.

Nowadays we might say, "Your opinion carries a lot of weight."

It's the same thing. We're old enough to remember "Jesus freaks" from the late 1960s who said, "God is heavy, man!" According to the Hebrew Scriptures, they weren't wrong.

In modern-day fireworks glory, this might be like the feeling of a veteran who served, say, in Vietnam and lost dear buddies on the battlefield. To him, the night sky filled with celebration is a glory with heavy weight, *kabod*.

Another image for glory emerged in Old Testament history—dazzling light. When Moses received the law on Mount Sinai, "to the Israelites the glory of the LORD looked like a consuming fire on top of the mountain" (Exodus 24:17). This fiery cloud moved ahead of the Israelites, guiding them as they traveled through the desert (Exodus 40:34–38; Numbers 9:15–22). It became known as God's presence (*shekinah* in Hebrew) and was often associated with his glory. When the Israelites' sacred tent was first used, it was covered by this bright cloud and "the glory of the LORD filled the tabernacle" (Exodus 40:34).

At the dedication of Solomon's temple, the worship service was cut short because this cloud was so dazzling.

> The trumpeters and musicians joined in unison to give praise and thanks to the LORD. Accompanied by trumpets, cymbals and other instruments, the singers raised their voices in praise to the LORD and sang:
>
> > "He is good;
> > his love endures forever."
>
> Then the temple of the LORD was filled with the cloud, and the priests could not perform their ser-

vice because of the cloud, for the glory of the LORD filled the temple of God. (2 Chronicles 5:13–14)

At various points in Israel's history, God demonstrated his presence in the cloud of his glory. Scripture also says that God's glory fills the whole earth (Numbers 14:21; Habakkuk 2:14), but at certain times and places, God seemed to set off fireworks to remind his people of his presence. "I am here. I will guide you. I am weighty."

So it makes perfect sense that the birth of "God with us," Emmanuel, the Bethlehem baby, is celebrated with a light show. An angel delivers the most important message ever, and then the sky blows up, with an army of angels singing God's praises. And what are they singing?

"Glory to God in the highest" (Luke 2:14).

In that moment, the heavens were declaring the glory of God in a way the psalmist could not have imagined. The God whose glory fills the earth was saying, "I have come to be with you."

Writing his gospel, John apparently decided to leave the Christmas story to his colleagues Matthew and Luke. He focused on how the adult Jesus interacted with people and shared his true identity. But John started with a remarkable intro.

Beginning with echoes of Genesis 1 ("In the beginning was the Word . . ."), by the time he gets to the pivotal verse 14, he might be thinking of Exodus.

"The Word became flesh and made his dwelling among us" (John 1:14). The word for "made his dwelling" literally means "pitched a tent"—the verb form of the noun used for the Israelites' tabernacle. But there's more.

"We have seen his glory, the glory of the one and only Son, who came from the Father, full of grace and truth" (v. 14).

Just as people had seen the glory of the Lord descending from heaven to fill the tabernacle of Israel, so John and others saw the only begotten Son of God bringing his glory to earth, pitching his tent among common folks and filling their lives.

This, too, is the Christmas story.

Preparing for Christmas

You might say *melisma* is the musical form of fireworks. It's defined as a single word or syllable sung over a sequence of notes. It's sometimes also called a vocal run.

You likely will recognize it best in the Christmas carol "Angels We Have Heard on High," its chorus of "Gloria!" sung in melisma over a soaring then cascading series of notes.

It's appropriate for you now, on Christmas Day, to sing "Gloria in excelsis Deo"—"Glory to God in the highest." Make your own fireworks for God. In this, acknowledge the fullest meaning of the season. Not just baby Jesus in a manger, not just angels and shepherds and wise men, not just prophecies fulfilled about the Messiah—as extraordinary as all that is. But the Christmas meaning that John conveys: how God through Jesus Christ has pitched his tent right beside yours. He is like you. Emmanuel. He is with you.

> *Lord God, I cannot begin to fathom your glory, but I come to you with joy for what you've done for me, for what the full meaning of Christmas really is. I praise you, Lord! Thank you for being with me.*

List of Songs and Carols

Each of the word-chapters in this book mentions a Christmas carol that connects to the theme. The music of these songs is utterly beautiful, and you may find it inspiring to listen as you use this book in your devotional time. We have created a playlist featuring many of these songs. You can access this playlist by searching for "The Wonder of Christmas" by Ken Petersen on Spotify.

In the Bleak Midwinter
The Boy's Dream
O Come, All Ye Faithful
Mary of the Incarnation
Hail to the Lord's Anointed

As with Gladness Men of Old
Brightest and Best of the Stars of the Morning
Joy Has Dawned (Across the World)
Coventry Carol
Silent Night

O Come, O Come, Emmanuel
At the Name of Jesus
We Three Kings
Where Shepherds Lately Knelt
O Little Town of Bethlehem

The Cherry Tree Carol
Away in a Manger
O Holy Night
For unto Us a Child Is Born
The First Noel

Mary, Did You Know?
Magnificat (Wexford Carol)
Joy to the World
The Incarnation
Angels We Have Heard on High

Notes

1. Taken from *The Message*, copyright © 1993, 2002, 2018 by Eugene H. Peterson. Used by permission of NavPress, represented by Tyndale House Publishers. All rights reserved.

2. Wayne Grudem, "Angels in the Bible: What Do We Actually Know about Them?," Zondervan Academic, December 13, 2017, https://zondervanacademic.com/blog/biblical-facts-angels.

3. Sinclair B. Ferguson, *Love Came Down at Christmas: Daily Readings for Advent* (Charlotte, NC: Good Book Company, 2018), 13.

4. Timothy Keller, *Hidden Christmas: The Surprising Truth behind the Birth of Christ* (New York: Penguin Publishing Group, 2018), 113.

5. "The Boy's Dream," in *Christmas Carols New and Old, Third Series*, ed. Henry Ramsden Bramley and John Stainer (London: Novello, Ewer & Co., 1878), 172–73.

6. A. W. Tozer, *Meditations on the Trinity: Beauty, Mystery, and the Glory in the Life of God* (Chicago: Moody Publishers, 2017), 68.

7. Rebecca McLaughlin, *Jesus through the Eyes of Women: How the First Female Disciples Help Us Know and Love the Lord* (Austin, TX: The Gospel Coalition, 2022), 25.

8. "Mary of the Incarnation," words by Christopher Idle © The Jubilate Group (Admin. Hope Publishing Company, www.hopepublishing.com). All rights reserved. Used by permission.

9. Ace Collins, *Stories behind the Great Traditions of Christmas* (Grand Rapids, MI: Zondervan, 2010), 184.

10. David and Barbara Leeman, *Hosanna in Excelsis: Hymns and Devotions for the Christmas Season* (Chicago: Moody Publishers, 2020), 104.

11. C. S. Lewis, *The Lion, the Witch and the Wardrobe* (New York: HarperCollins, 1978), 19. First published 1950.

12. "Joy Has Dawned (Across the World)," Stuart Townend and Keith Getty Copyright © 2005 Thankyou Music Ltd (PRS) (adm. worldwide at CapitolCMGPublishing.com excluding the UK & Europe which is adm. at IntegratedRights.com). All rights reserved. Used by permission.

13. William Shakespeare, *Hamlet*, Folger Shakespeare Library, ed. Barbara A. Mowat and Paul Werstine (New York: Simon & Schuster, 2012), 137. First published 1603.

14. Collins, *Stories behind the Great Traditions of Christmas*, 126.

15. John Piper, "O Come, O Come, Emmanuel," Desiring God, December 13, 2015, https://www.desiringgod.org/articles/o-come-o-come-emmanuel.

16. Billy Sunday, "Wonderful," in Elijah P. Brown, *The Real Billy Sunday: The Life and Work of Rev. William Ashley Sunday, D.D., the Baseball Evangelist* (New York: Fleming H. Revell Company, 1914), 272.

17. Taken from the Good News Translation in Today's English Version—Second Edition Copyright © 1992 by American Bible Society. Used by permission.

18. Where Shepherds Lately Knelt, Verse 1 by Jaroslav J. Vajda © 1986 Concordia Publishing House. Used with permission. cph.org.

19. Phillips Brooks, *Letters of Travel* (New York: E. P. Dutton & Co., 1893), 69.

20. Russell Moore, "Father to God, Model for Us," The Gospel Coalition, December 15, 2011, https://www.thegospelcoalition.org/article/father-to-god-model-for-us/.

21. Barbara Robinson, *The Best Christmas Pageant Ever* (New York: HarperCollins, 1972), 1, 39, 43.

22. Saint Bonaventure, *The Life of Saint Francis*, trans. E. Gurney Salter (London: J. M. Dent and Company, 1904), 111.

23. Ace Collins, "The Amazing Story of 'O Holy Night,'" BeliefNet, accessed December 28, 2022, https://www.beliefnet.com/entertainment/movies/the-nativity-story/the-amazing-story-of-o-holy-night.aspx.

24. "John Sullivan Dwight," Virtual American Biographies, accessed December 28, 2022, http://www.famousamericans.net/johnsullivandwight/.

25. Mark Lowry, "Mary, Did You Know?" (Nashville: Word Music and Rufus Music, 1991).

26. Keith and Kristyn Getty, "Magnificat (with Wexford Carol) – Keith & Kristyn Getty," tranceseraph, November 1, 2011, video, 4:51, https://www.youtube.com/watch?v=Z6nAsESYPiY.

27. R. C. Sproul, "Incarnation," in *What Did Jesus Do? Understanding the Work of Christ*, Ligonier Ministries, accessed December 30, 2022, video, 23:51, https://www.ligonier.org/learn/series/what-did-jesus-do.

28. Henry Ramsden Bramley, "The Incarnation," in *Christmas Carols New and Old Series*, ed. Henry Ramsden Bramley and John Stainer (London: Novello, Ewer and Co., 1871), 57.

Spread the Word
by Doing One Thing.

- Give a copy of this book as a gift.
- Share the QR code link via your social media.
- Write a review of this book on your blog, favorite bookseller's website, or at ODB.org/store.
- Recommend this book to your church, small group, or book club.